Praise for *Death by Baptism*

"Frank Honeycutt's exploration is a masterful piece of pastoral theology—no, pastoral baptismal theology—that courageously starts where Paul starts, with fear and death. He plunges us into a wide range of authors who become sources of insight in pastoral care and preaching while keeping sacramental formation in view. *Death by Baptism* will stimulate pastoral reflection for years to come."

—Scot McKnight, professor of New
Testament at Northern Seminary

"When I want to think clearly and imaginatively about baptism, I go to a Lutheran for help. We couldn't have a better guide than Lutheran pastor / writer Frank Honeycutt. *Death by Baptism* is a remarkable book that can help any Christian find new meaning and significance in the sacrament of Christian initiation. 'Remember your baptism and be thankful,' we pastors say to our people. Frank's evocative book will help you do just that."

—Will Willimon, professor of Christian ministry and
United Methodist bishop, retired, and author of
Leading with the Sermon: Preaching as Leadership

"With characteristic honesty and humor, Frank Honeycutt shares the kind of wisdom that only an experienced parish pastor can provide. In a time when countless voices are clamoring to make us feel fractured and fearful, Frank offers a word of hope soaked in the waters of baptism. We have already died. So how, then, will we now live?"

—Christa Compton, pastor at Gloria Dei
Lutheran Church, Chatham, NJ

"Teeming with unpretentious wisdom and rich biblical insight, *Death by Baptism* calls the church to rediscover and remain faithful to the liberating power of its radical baptismal identity. This is a must read for clergy looking to reestablish a relevant and vital sacramental foundation for their ministries. Vintage Honeycutt!"

—Wayne Kannaday, professor of
religion at Newberry College

"Frank Honeycutt achieves the remarkable: he talks so effectively about baptism's power to free us from fear that the book itself becomes a journey of liberation, a loosening of the fetters of fear. In effecting what it talks about, *Death by Baptism* reflects the special power of the sacraments to do what they say."

—John F. Hoffmeyer, associate professor of systematic
theology at United Lutheran Seminary

death by
baptism

death by baptism

SACRAMENTAL LIBERATION
IN A CULTURE OF FEAR

FRANK G. HONEYCUTT

Fortress Press
Minneapolis

DEATH BY BAPTISM
Sacramental Liberation in a Culture of Fear

Cover image: Vishal Banik / Unsplash
Cover design: John M. Lucas

Print ISBN: 978-1-5064-7004-7
eBook ISBN: 978-1-5064-7005-4

In loving memory of my mother,
father, and "little brother"

~~~~~

Ruth Gaines Honeycutt
1930–2017

~~~~~

Robert Lee Honeycutt Jr.
1926–2018

~~~~~

Lee Barnhardt Honeycutt
1959–2019

Contents

Acknowledgments

I'm grateful to the following kind folk for research advice, manuscript feedback, and/or general encouragement as this book took shape: Cindy Honeycutt, Ron Luckey, Bill Gable, Rhonda Kindig, John Lang, John Gifford, Michael Kohn, Howard and Tina Pillot, Julian Gordy, Tony Metze, Tom Ward, Chris Lawrence, Paul Pingel, Pat Riddle, Sandy Leach, Lukas Honeycutt, Rachel Connelly, Chris Heavner, and Larry Harley.

Introduction

TREASURE IN CLAY JARS

During an extended drought in book three of C. S. Lewis's Narnia series, *The Voyage of the Dawn Treader*, an obnoxious child steals water carefully rationed among his shipmates. Eustace becomes so self-centered that he eventually turns into a dragon and grows scales, giving in to the greed of all that glitters, isolated on an island away from the ship. In pain from the constriction of a gold bracelet, he tries three times to scratch off the scaly skin, but it grows back.

Aslan the Lion locates Eustace in his isolation and offers an invitation packed with baptismal implications. Aslan says, "You will have to let me undress you." Eustace describes what happens next:

> The very first tear he made was so deep that I thought it had gone right to my heart. And when he began pulling the skin off, it hurt worse than anything I've ever felt. . . . Then he caught hold of me and threw me into the water. It smarted like anything but only for a moment. After that it became delicious and as soon as I started swimming and splashing, I found that all the pain had gone from my arm. And then I saw why. I'd turned into a boy again.[1]

In baptism, we are given a new identity, a different perspective on living in the world. We die to an old life, crucified with Christ (Gal 2:20)—we become a new creation (2 Cor 5:17). Disciples are freed from the great fear of death by *going ahead and dying* before we breathe our last breath. If we've already died, the paralyzing apprehension of such a day diminishes.

As a Lutheran pastor for over three decades, I've led many church classes inviting participants to offer various images that come to mind upon hearing the word *baptism*. Groups suggest valid and biblical responses: new life, rebirth, cleansing, forgiveness, family, body of Christ.

However, the word *death*—a central reality describing the sacrament in the New Testament—rarely receives mention:

> Do you not know that all of us who have been baptized into Christ Jesus were baptized into his death? Therefore we have been buried with him by baptism into death, so that, just as Christ was raised from the dead by the glory of the Father, so we too might walk in newness of life. For if we have been united with him in a death like his, we will certainly be united with him in a resurrection like his. (Rom 6:3–5)

Saint Paul's rather jarring declaration is no biblical anomaly: "You have died, and your life is hidden with Christ in God" (Col 3:3); "When you were buried with him in baptism, you were also raised with him through faith in the power of God" (Col 12:2); "I have been crucified with Christ; and it is no longer I who live, but it is Christ who lives in me" (Gal 2:19–20).

Elaborate sermons on dying in baptism were once preached in the early church. The Red Sea story in Exodus became symbolic of how baptism drowns the pursuit of sin and the old life in Egypt, washing up a new community of people on the far shore of a whole new land.

Popular at one time in church history was a tomb-like function for baptismal fonts. Catechumens baptized in the font of Saint Ambrose (340–97) in Milan descended precipitous steps into water with depth, dying into Christ's body (the church), and ascended steps out the other side to a waiting congregation and first communion. Martin Luther preferred full immersion in the waters of the font, even with small children, to suggest a visual dying and rising with Christ—a drowning, a death, a new creation.[2] This liquid drenching is in rather stark contrast to the minimal use of water in many churches today in what has been whimsically called a "dry cleaning."

The connection between death and baptism is rather murky in much of the church today. *That baby is just too cute! So full of life and curls and dimples.* Innocence clouds our thinking. The sacrament often becomes more about family tradition, photo opportunities, and even a fuzzy and misguided notion of fire insurance, a magical protection from a hellish afterlife. I've received more than a few frantic phone calls from mothers who ask, "Will you do my baby?" Desiring to maintain evangelical inclusion, pastorally raising the connection between death and baptism is a challenge under such circumstances without scaring away a prospective member of the congregation.

In many parts of Central America (a region where death and violence are daily realities), the priest and other family members somberly process into a darkened nave wearing funeral garb as worshippers intone songs of lament and loss. At the altar, the priest plunges the naked child completely underwater into a wooden font shaped like a funeral casket and says, "I *kill* you in the name of the Father, Son, and Holy Spirit . . . and raise you to walk in Christ's light and love forever!"

Postbaptism, the congregation dramatically shifts to songs of Easter praise. The dripping-wet child is garbed with a white baptismal gown and screams like she's just been born—an apt image.[3] Try this just once in your home congregation and somebody will call the Department of Social Services.

To our great theological impoverishment, the church has largely lost the core image of dying with Christ in celebrating the sacrament of baptism. Saint Paul uses the word *death* (or its close cousins) *fourteen times* in the first eleven verses of Romans 6.

I counted.

~~~~~~~~

Baptism is not some holy inoculation protecting disciples from evil and mishap. Jesus proceeds directly from his baptism in the Jordan River, barely toweled off, to an immediate encounter with the devil in the wilderness (Mark 1:9–13). Apparently, this ancient sacrament fails to magically protect Jesus or his followers, chosen recipients of God's promises, from whatever's "out there." Baptism instead provides the church with the spiritual wherewithal to confront and talk back to sin and evil. Dying with Christ in baptism suggests a powerful truth: *nothing can "get" us—God's already got us.*

For several years I've been inspired (and baptismally haunted) by a story that occurred in El Salvador outside the small village of El Mozote during the country's long and violent civil war (1980–92).[4] The story describes a young girl, sexually assaulted by soldiers, whose bravery undoubtedly found its origin through her watery death in Christ that occurred years before, shaping an identity unassailable even by unspeakable brutality:

> There was [a girl] the soldiers talked about . . . whom they had raped many times during the course of the afternoon, and through it all, while the other women of El Mozote had screamed and cried . . . this girl had sung hymns, strange evangelical songs, and she had kept right on singing, even after they had done what had to be done and shot her in the chest. She had lain there on La Cruz with the blood flowing from her chest and had kept on singing—a bit weaker than before, but still singing. And the soldiers, stupefied, had watched and pointed. Then they had grown tired of the game and shot her

again, and she sang still, and their wonder began to turn to fear—until finally they unsheathed their machetes and hacked through her neck, and at last the singing stopped.[5]

I suspect few North American pastors will ever face darkness quite this palpable. But here's a ministerial hunch: until congregations start celebrating the "death date" in baptism at least as vigorously as we celebrate our planetary debuts, our corporate ability to be church together in the world (and our sacramental wherewithal to stare down evil) will be severely stunted and diminished.

"Our rituals," writes Gabe Huck, "are a kind of rehearsal. What are we rehearsing? In that cross traced over and over, we are learning the very shape of our lives, knowing or absorbing little by little how for us that cross is the weapon against evil and the victory over death."[6]

Who am I? Steeped in the traditions of the Old South, I indeed debuted as a Tennessean born to Ruth and Bob Honeycutt on May 15, 1957, at Memorial Hospital in downtown Chattanooga. A certain family, a unique region dripping with history within a relatively still-new nation.

These undeniable shapers of my personality and passions, these three realities (genealogy, regional identity, national citizenship) do not describe my primary identity. I died on a hot summer Sunday—July 28 of that same year—when Pastor Jim Cadwallader poured water on my bald baby head and told me I was a Christian. I died that day and have been swimming around in the grace of God ever since. (Sometimes dog paddling, I'll admit.)

"Don't you know . . . Don't you know that all of us who have been baptized into Christ Jesus were baptized into his death?"

There are few more poignant questions in the entire Bible. Now that we've gotten death out of the way and behind us, who knows what risky lives God has in store?

Nothing can get you out there in the shadowy future. Jesus knows your head better than any barber (Matt 10:30). He sleeps peacefully on a boat cushion during a storm while the disciples are largely losing it (Mark 4:35–41).

You've *already* died. You've been claimed by Christ. The perfect love poured into our lives at baptism casts out all fear (1 John 4:18).

~~~~~~~

Christians have lived for centuries in cultures where fear and worry have shaped political trends with emergent messiahs preying upon various vulnerabilities among those who pray.[7] Instead of succumbing to the false promises of a temporary savior, the early church and its leaders offered a different proclamation even in the midst of agonizing afflictions, perplexities, and persecutions:

For we do not proclaim ourselves; we proclaim Jesus Christ as Lord and ourselves as your slaves for Jesus' sake. For it is the God who said, "Let light shine out of darkness," who has shone in our hearts to give the light of the knowledge of the glory of God in the face of Jesus Christ. But we have this treasure in clay jars, so that it may be made clear that this extraordinary power belongs to God and does not come from us. We are afflicted in every way, but not crushed; perplexed, but not driven to despair; persecuted, but not forsaken; struck down, but not destroyed; always carrying in the body the death of Jesus, so that the life of Jesus may also be made visible in our bodies. (2 Cor 4:5–10)

This book, written for pastors (and worship leaders) searching for a deeper understanding of baptism, seeks to reveal how "always carrying in the body the death of Jesus" offers parishioners an identity capable of withstanding any threat or fear—national or personal—that might afflict seemingly fragile "clay jars" like any of us. Each chapter will explore aspects of pastoral ministry from the perspective of a body of people who've already died and risen in Christ through ancient sacramental promises.

In Alice McDermott's powerful novel *The Ninth Hour*, a young woman named Sally eventually determines that life in a convent is not for her. The press of so much misery upon nuns in early twentieth-century Brooklyn steers her toward a more settled and predictable employment in a local tearoom. This decision, ultimately, is not so peaceful:

> She walked home after work, in the cold darkness, under streetlamps encircled with fog. How would she live, having seen what she had seen? It had been one thing to refuse the convent, to say, "I've thought better of it," after the long train ride showed her the truth of the dirty world, showed her that her own impulse was to meet its filthy citizens not with a consoling cloth, but with a curse, a punch in the face. But now it was life itself she wanted to refuse, for how could she live knowing that stillness, that inconsequence, that feral smell of death, was what her days were aiming her toward?[8]

My own pastoral ministry was marked by many encounters with people not all that different from Sally, fearful of death and paralyzed by the dread of it. I've encountered good and faithful people who've seen and experienced unspeakable tragedy and now seek to manage and prevent suffering in the future through means that may compete, at least temporarily, with the promises of Jesus.

The chapters that follow seek to answer an old question for the church in a new era of fear. How does baptism shape an identity utterly confident in Christ regardless of external circumstance or national threat? If we've already died, "undressed" like Eustace and clothed with the promises of Christ, how shall we now live?

1

Fear in Parish Life

Healer of our ev'ry ill, light of each tomorrow,
give us peace beyond our fear, and hope beyond
our sorrow.

—MARTY HAUGEN

Near Tampa many years ago for a conference exploring modern implications of the historic catechumenate (the ancient protracted process preparing adult candidates for baptism), I heard a story offered by an Episcopal bishop who described a congregation—near the Smokies in the mountains of East Tennessee—within his diocese and general oversight.[1]

Due to a shrinking membership census, the congregation was served by seminary interns in a succession of one-year stints. One seminarian, poring over past sacramental history in the church archives, came upon an entry with a name, date, and cryptic two-word comment alongside an eye-catching asterisk: "Grover Crockett*, Partially Baptized."

Perplexed, salvifically vigilant, and more than a little curious, the seminary intern (I'll call her Ginny) phoned her pastoral supervisor thirty miles away. "Ask around," he said. "You're not there for very long, but part of this year is learning how to become something of a clergy sleuth. I suspect there's an interesting story among your older parishioners."

Vicar Ginny visited Milt and Garnett—both born near the church and married in the sanctuary—who recalled Grover, then in his late eighties, who'd never been baptized but grew up in the Baptist tradition. He wanted to be baptized during the Easter season and fully immersed in the creek that ran below the church building.

Easter came early that year. "About as early as it could possibly fall," Milt said.

"Late March," said Garnett. "On the second Sunday of the season, after a stirring sermon about that rascal Thomas, my favorite disciple, most of the congregation hiked down the hill and assembled on the creek bank. It was a warm day in early April, but let me tell you, that water was cold from snow-melt from way up in the national park."

"Our pastor at the time wore fishing waders for the baptism," Milt continued. "Old Grover went all the way under once and then again, holding his nose throughout. Nobody so much as coughed. It was pretty dramatic and all."

"When he came up that second time, though, sputtering and shaking," Garnett said, "you could have heard Grover yell all the way up to Clingman's Dome. That old man was practically running, yelling, as he made for the creek bank and a dry towel."

Milt and Garnett looked at Vicar Ginny and quoted Grover's chilly groan in unison:

"The Father and Son were hard enough. I can't take the Holy Spirit!"

~~~~~~

In her short story "The River" (first published in 1955), Flannery O'Connor writes about a young boy, Harry Ashfield, whose need to belong to something larger than his strange family causes him to deceive his new babysitter, Mrs. Connin, and adopt the first name of a local preacher, Bevel Summers, who draws crowds to an "old red water river" where people come for baptism outside an unnamed Southern town. Harry/Bevel walks to the river one day with Mrs. Connin, a fervent believer, and decides to come forward for the sacrament:

> "Have you ever been Baptized?" the preacher asked.
>
> "What's that?" he murmured.
>
> "If I baptize you," the preacher said, "you'll be able to go to the Kingdom of Christ. You'll be washed in the river of suffering, son, and you'll go by the deep river of life. Do you want that?"
>
> "Yes," the child said, and thought, I won't go back to the apartment then; I'll go under the river.
>
> "You won't be the same again," the preacher said. "You'll count." . . . He held him under while he said the words of Baptism and then he jerked him up again and looked sternly at the gasping child . . . "You count now," the preacher said. "You didn't even count before."
>
> The little boy was too shocked to cry. He spit out the muddy water and rubbed his wet sleeve into his eyes and over his face.[2]

A bevel in carpentry is "a sloping surface." The arc of the story suggests this preacher (and the boy) may indeed be on a theologically slippery slope in their understanding of baptism. The babysitter's last name reveals Flannery's own theological suspicions that many of her regional kindred are "conned" by promises of a false identity composed of now "counting" in the Lord's eyes only as a result of baptism. It's also entirely possible that the similarity of the writer's own last name to Mrs. Connin's may reveal Flannery's own sometimes silent complicity in such an understanding. O'Connor was a savvy and committed Roman Catholic churchgoer her entire adult life before succumbing to lupus at age thirty-nine. She also was well aware of the flaws and foibles of the church and local theology applied misguidedly.[3] O'Connor deftly recognized that the Christian vision in her stories, addressed to a culture that increasingly did not share this vision, should often be administered "by shock—to the hard of hearing you shout, and for the almost-blind you draw large and startling figures."[4] In her novel *The Violent Bear It Away* (1960), a baptism shockingly results in an actual drowning.

A parish pastor for thirty-one years in four different locales—rural, small town, and urban settings—I received more than one frantic phone call from a worried parent eager to schedule the sacrament lest some dark event might befall their child. This lingering perception of the sacrament suggests magical inclusion, a protective shield from all evil, and minimal understanding of baptism's biblical purpose.

"What's that?" the child asks of baptism in O'Connor's story. According to Rev. Bevel Summers (and many other clergy of my acquaintance still mired in a missionary understanding that once fueled arduous journeys across the world primarily initiated to save heathens from hell), baptism is centrally a "counting" exercise and little more.

I can't take the Holy Spirit. Perhaps Grover Crockett's amusing "partial" dunking unintentionally reveals what's truly at stake in baptism with a Spirit that brings "a new creation" (2 Cor 5:17) into being whose identity is so grounded in the promises of the Holy Trinity that any threat, any fear (future or present) is given relative and persistent demotion in a believer's daily existence.

If this is indeed a central part of the Holy Spirit's job description, as I intend to clarify in these pages, then such a dunking for many can be quite a lot to "take." Relying on God rather than myriad supplemental protections may indeed cause one to run like hell toward the hills with Grover. But such a radical identity can also certainly form an enviable "peace of God, which surpasses all understanding" (Phil 4:7), guarding the hearts and minds of the baptized to face any obstacle or perceived threat.

I'm thinking here of the amazing peace and calm exhibited by Paul and Silas, who land in prison after healing a soothsaying slave girl (Acts 16:16–40) possessed by "a spirit of divination" (16:16).[5] Her mother may have been happy after the healing, but the Chamber of Commerce is livid. For Philippi, a town only a couple miles from the Aegean Sea with a fair number of seafaring tourists, the girl was something of an economic boon.

Money isn't funny. People vote with their pocketbooks, then and now. Two disruptive pastors—perhaps emboldened from a fresh encounter with Lydia and other converts down by the river (16:13) in the local congregation's origin story—are perceived as threats to the local economy, "disturbing our city" (16:20). Paul and Silas are stripped naked, beaten with rods, and placed "in the innermost cell" (16:24) of the prison with their feet in stocks—basically "under the jail" as my public defender daughter puts it when she visits clients who've really messed up.

I (a sometimes-jaded pastor) can imagine any number of jaded responses from these two river preachers with bloodied backs and nobody to call. Instead, around midnight, "Paul and Silas were praying and singing hymns to God"[6] (16:25) in a surprising choral testimony to other prisoners listening nearby. God apparently heard them also. An earthquake liberates the two pastors and the entire inmate population, but you really have to conclude that the hymn-singers possessed an enviable freedom long before the chains fell off. Their true liberation resided in an identity capable of withstanding this or any bruising, bloody night that might come their way.

This truth is underscored, in contrast, by the reaction of the jailer, roused from the rumbling, who comes close to dying by suicide (16:27) upon discovering (on his watch) a seemingly empty jail. The man holding all the keys to the place—jangling in his pocket, surely reminding him who was in charge—is actually in bondage to great fear and trepidation, under the thumb of another perceived power. It's a delicious literary twist and conjures several important questions: *Who in this story is really free? Who is imprisoned by what? What ultimate power truly holds the keys to liberation?*

Please note that the jailbirds make no attempt to escape postearthquake. Give credit to the jailer, moved by the events of this night, for asking the right question: "Sirs, what must I do to be saved?" (16:30)—a loaded evangelical question, centuries later, but here having loads more to do with this life than the next. The man could have put it another way: "How in the world can I discover in my fear-filled life the freedom you two seem to presently have in yours?"

Paul and Silas reveal the true keeper of the keys to this frightened man and all in his household. The water used to wash pastoral wounds (16:33) undoubtedly flowed from the same local spring used that night for the baptisms of the jailer and his entire family.[7] Unlike the superficial sacramental benefit espoused by Rev. Bevel Summers in O'Connor's short story, these two river preachers share a gift with a spiritual depth far beyond "counting" new souls magically added to a faraway promised place.[8] Paul and Silas are so secure in their conviction concerning the true possessor of the keys to freedom that they *still* make no attempt to flee the premises but decide to hang around until the next morning to confront the very men who bloodied their backs (16:37–39). Only then do they return to the relative safety of the home (16:40) of their early church council leader, Lydia, who sold purple cloth (16:14) and perhaps took note that some of her colorful cloth ironically matched their raised bruises.

It's natural for modern Christians to perhaps ponder with some envy the bravery of Paul and Silas and pose the understandable question of the man who jangled all the keys in his pocket: *What must I do to get what you've got?* Future chapters of this book will address *how* pastors and local congregations might shape a vigorous process of Christian formation resulting in a holy confidence similar to these two jailed pastors. For now, however, I want to linger with this jailer; his initial fear and its paralysis are mirrored in the lives of many church people of my acquaintance.

~~~~~~

> Women received their dead by resurrection. Others were tortured, refusing to accept release, in order to obtain a better resurrection. Others suffered mocking and flogging, and even chains and imprisonment. They were stoned to death, they were sawn in two, they were killed by the sword; they went about in skins of sheep and goats, destitute, persecuted, tormented—of whom the world was not worthy. They wandered in deserts and mountains, and in caves and holes in the ground.
>
> —HEBREWS 11:35–38

People of faith have historically resided in a world full of violence, unexpected disease, and various maladies associated with aging.[9] I suspect at least part of the spike in personal and corporate fear (along with the erosion of ultimate trust) among baptized Christians early in the twenty-first century—and the accompanying advance of protection devices ranging from gun technology to home surveillance gizmos—finds a direct correlation in the rapid increase in general life expectancy over the last fifty years.

Followers of Jesus know that life generally has a finite term limit,[10] but medical and health discoveries have undeniably extended the sense that we'll all live appreciably longer than our forebears, postponing conversations about death and common mortality far into the future, if indeed they ever occur at all.

Sherwin Nuland, a doctor and writer who admits that he knows better, describes his family's reaction to the approaching death of his beloved Aunt Rose: "It was like the old scenario that so often throws a shadow over the last days of people with cancer: we knew—she knew—we knew she knew—she knew we knew—and none of us would talk about it when we were all together. We kept up the charade until the end."[11]

My father, a wonderful man and active each Sunday in his Lutheran church choir for decades, surprised me a bit on a visit. My mom had died in the previous year. Several health setbacks left Dad largely confined to a wheelchair and under the care of an excellent nursing staff in a nearby residential facility—about the best possible outcome given the circumstances. One day, as it often did, the conversation drifted to a litany of his health woes. "I never thought this would happen to me," he said, with head in hands. My brothers and I sometimes smiled about my father's penchant for "the single" (head resting in one hand) or "the double" (head in both hands). This was decidedly a day for the double. "What *did* you think would happen?" the pastor-son (*c'est moi*) inquired. "I don't know," Dad replied. "*Not this.*"

My wife, Cindy, and I were heading somewhere special recently, a rare date out, both of us standing in front of the bathroom mirror preparing to depart. "Which of us do you think will die first?" I asked, out of the blue. "I don't know, but I hope it's you," she said. "Why would you say that?" I responded, rather stunned. "Because," Cindy replied, "women handle the death of a spouse better than men." She's generally right, I suspect.

The sisterly reaction to their brother's death in John's Gospel, however, suggests mortality paralysis is not gender specific. Martha and Mary each confront their friend Jesus on the road and levy a duplicate and rather brassy accusation not long after Lazarus's demise: "Lord, if you had been here, my brother would not have died" (John 11:21, 32).

Their words here serve as an honest internal gut check for many (including myself) whose emotions at untimely death are almost closer to anger than grief. It's not hard to imagine what the sisters were really thinking—maybe this chastising internal zinger: *"If you'd gotten off your ass, Jesus, if you'd stopped screwing around with your pals for almost a week after you first heard the news, my brother would be with us right now. Where were you?"*

Jesus is indeed hopelessly late to Bethany. (The town's literal meaning is "House of Affliction," curiously.) Lazarus has been entombed four days (11:17) when Jesus finally shows up, even though he was fully aware of his friend's illness early on (11:4–6). Mary and Martha speak for anyone who wonders about the seeming absence of the divine in the face of tragedy. The neighbors, similar to a community Greek chorus, drive home an honest follow-up question: "Could not he who opened the eyes of the blind man have kept this man from dying?" (11:37).

> It's a fair question that echoes over millennia, not to mention the lips of my own agnostic friends. If Jesus has it in him to still wind and wave, why does he allow earthquakes and tsunamis? If he fed 5,000 with a little boy's little lunch, why does anyone go to bed hungry at night? If he healed that blind guy down the road, why doesn't he show up here in Bethany and work his magic? The neighborly chorus reflects questions of theodicy as old as Job.[12]

Jesus may be late for his friend's funeral, but upon arrival, he walks right toward death. Note his confident impatience with Martha: "Did I not tell you that if you believed, you would see the glory of God?" (11:40). *Have I not mentioned this already?* His terse prayer in front of the tomb also reveals frustration with the gathered mourners: "I knew that you always hear me, but I have said this for the sake of the crowd standing here" (11:42).

For the sake of these theological dullards, he seems to pray, curtly. Jesus reminds me of the preacher who continues to take potshots at the congregation in his or her postsermon intercessions. (For the record, there's a good chance Jesus might have failed pastoral care had he taken such a course in seminary. The man is no hand-holder or ambassador of etiquette, especially in John's Gospel.)

Lazarus eventually comes forth like a walking mummy, tomb-wrappings trailing along behind. Jesus's words here are telling: "Unbind him, and let him go" (11:44). He could just as easily have said, "Unbind *them,* and let them go." That is, liberate the fearful community from their great and paralyzing apprehension of death.

Appallingly tardy, Jesus refuses to be pulled hither and yon by death in this old story, refuses to be jerked around by death's timetable. He does not permit death to drive the action, dictate his pastoral response, or shape his emotions. He does famously weep (11:35), but his anger on either side of the tears (11:33, 38)[13] suggests much more occurring here than sadness alone.

Jesus offers a rather befuddling statement early in this old story. Upon receiving a message from the sisters concerning his friend's malady, the Lord says with a physician's air of confidence, "This illness does not lead to death" (11:4). Since Lazarus certifiably croaks down the way, one must conclude that either Jesus has just offered a classic medical misdiagnosis or something else is going on. (In John's Gospel, of course, theological polyvalence and double entendres abound.)

The coronavirus (COVID-19) pandemic is sweeping across the globe as I write these words, with many documented deaths and outbreaks of the illness. One is left wondering if Jesus would offer a similar assessment concerning this virus that has left much of the world paralyzed in fear. Such an assessment begs the question, *If this illness doesn't lead to death, Jesus, then what indeed does?* In short (his actions seem to reveal in this story), our paralyzing apprehension of death.

A careful reader of this narrative recalls connections reminiscent of the Philippian jailer who senses a power in Paul and Silas that exceeds any perceived fear. Bethany is just two miles from Jerusalem (John 11:18) and a hill with a cross that grafts the baptized into the death and resurrection of Jesus (Rom 6:3–5), signing and shaping the lives of his followers. Fill an empty tomb with water and you've got yourself a baptismal font.[14] We've already died in Christ. Failing to embrace this powerful theological reality—mired in great fear of the day when we stop breathing—is indeed the "illness" that currently paralyzes Christ's church.

Unbind us, Lord. Let us go.

~~~~~~

"Real power is, I don't ever want to use the word, *fear*," Donald Trump once opined.[15] Exploiting such fear drives recent elections, creates intense suspicion of the stranger, arms a nation with more guns per capita than any country in the world, and causes "loved ones" to resort to extreme medical measures rather than accept the reality of shared mortality. This is especially striking given the abundant appearance of the imperative "fear not" in the Bible—used seventy-five times in the Old Testament alone[16] and regularly found on the lips of angelic messengers featured in favorite nativity narratives.

In the church, such widespread fear suggests a theological crisis accompanied by a lack of biblical depth and cloaked doubts about any promise of life beyond this one, generating an astonishing variety of doomsday preppers, conspiracy theorists, and others consistently mired in the surpassing wisdom of the internet who all may well find a place in Sunday pews, seeking some additional talismanic direction to supplement well-formed suspicions. The Bible, of course, is not a totem touched periodically to mine magical power and protection. The Bible, used in trust, is a spiritual road map—when opened, read, and consulted with more regularity than, say, a television, newspaper, or president—for any Christian interested in courageously confronting and talking back to fear.

I've worked with church council leaders who had difficulty articulating the difference between the books of Exodus and Acts but somehow rose to a leadership position in the congregation due to perceived charisma among peer communicants. Is it any wonder that many Christians have allowed false political voices to articulate what they should fear as national citizens and how to respond? In 1967, over a half century ago, theologian, attorney, and activist William Stringfellow penned these prophetic and eerily prescient observations about the church's interaction with God's word:

> The weirdest corruption of contemporary American Protestantism is the virtual abandonment of the Word of God in the Bible. That is ironic because access to the Bible and devotion to the Word of God in the Bible was that out of which authentic Protestantism came into being. . . . Nowadays Protestants in America are neither intimate with nor reliant upon the Word of God in the Bible, whether in preaching, in services in the sanctuaries, or in education and nurture. Yet it is the Word of God in the Bible that all Christians are particularly called to hear, witness, trust, honor, and love. It is only in that Word that Protestantism can have either vivacity or probity anymore.[17]

This book will not degenerate into an extended diatribe against Donald Trump and his supporters. He's been likened to King Cyrus, pagan liberator of God's people from an extended exile in Babylon. "For the sake of my servant Jacob, and Israel my chosen, I call you by your name, I surname you, though you do not know me," God says of Cyrus (Isa 45:4). I somewhat understand the desire of his supporters to find any biblical proof for the ascendancy of Trump's shameless behavior, but I also honestly observe nothing of Jesus's teachings in King Donald, one who lives so little of the New Testament on a practically daily basis that his election by a Christian plurality still leaves me stunned most mornings and ready to plaster Stringfellow's charge on the front doors of churches across the land, Protestant or otherwise. If moral character is a basic condition for national leadership, Christians who overwhelmingly supported this president (largely due to fear) seem to not know (or care about) what centuries of their faith forebears taught, preached, and lived on the subject of something as basic as the fruit of the spirit—love, joy, peace, patience, kindness, generosity, faithfulness, gentleness, and self-control (Gal 5:22). Stringfellow's choice of the word *abandonment* is quite appropriate in our current Christian context. It's worth noting that his following reflection on placing death in its proper theological place was written in a time of great upheaval, change, violence, and fear (1964), gripping a nation struggling with civil and human rights. Knowing Stringfellow's larger body of work, I'm certain these words were addressed both to those bravely struggling for such rights and to those who resisted such change. They still speak to the church today:

> [Christ's] power over death is effective not just at the terminal point of a person's life but throughout one's life, during *this* life in *this* world, right now. This power is effective in the times and places in the daily lives of human beings when they are so gravely and relentlessly assailed by the claims of principalities for an idolatry that, in spite of all disguises, really surrenders to death as the reigning presence in the world. His resurrection

means the possibility of living in this life, in the very midst of death's works, safe and free from death.[18]

Fear often has a rather warped effect on Christian memory, creating a need to feel safe with a strong man and baptismally "protected," just in case, from evil and change (*Will you do my baby?*) and perhaps driven by a sinking suspicion that God seems to have left the premises. The night boat crossing with Jesus and his disciples in Mark 4:35–41, to which I now turn, is filled with details that speak to the source of our modern fears.

~~~~~~~

I live in a small town (population four thousand) in upstate South Carolina whose residents include a variety of creatures, even the occasional backyard bear. We're not far from the Chattooga River (a national scenic waterway) and enjoy the forty nearby waterfalls created by the ancient and precipitous Blue Ridge escarpment, gravity, and an inventive God.

On a recent bicycle ride along my daily route, I encountered a dead deer in the roadway's tall border grass and startled the eleven turkey vultures (I counted as they retreated to perches in nearby trees) who'd settled into a communal repast before my interruption. I stopped, got off the bike, and gave thanks for the deer's life that ended early that morning, as far as I could tell, probably the victim of an encounter with a car traveling too fast. The prayer was punctuated by the blare of a siren on the highway a quarter mile away, heading to a recent local mishap, and the gurgling of a nearby creek.

Returning to the scene late that afternoon on an errand in my car, I was astonished to discover how quickly the vultures had reduced the deer carcass to a rack of bones. A disembodied leg with a perfect black hoof was several feet away, its current placement on the pavement undoubtedly the result of an avian tussle over the fleshy leftovers. I rolled down the window and stared, entranced, and again heard the nearby creek. Tennyson's famous line about nature being "red in tooth and claw" swam through my imagination. I drove up a nearby hill toward the store with my grocery list and thought of a friend who was walking through her backyard one sunny day, nowhere near a tree. Half of a headless, bloody black snake dropped out of the sky and landed at her feet, almost causing Rhonda to jump out of her shoes. She heard a hawk call high above and concluded the bird would probably still be pleased with most of its to-go lunch. Death is all around us.

Even so, in baptism, "God has not given us a spirit of fear, but of power and of love and of a sound mind" (2 Tim 1:7 NKJV). I love this verse and trust its promises, especially as I hear the tumbling of water in nearby rivers and creeks on various recreational forays, musical baptismal reminders of a powerful common identity capable of withstanding grave threat, darkness, and death itself: "There is a river whose streams make glad the city of God, the holy habitation of the Most High" (Ps 46:4). The myriad streams and rivulets of denominational expression and spiritual practice through the centuries of Christianity compose a great river flowing toward an unshakeable realm of peace. The lifeboat of the church floats on the waters of promise toward an indescribable reality of love and justice for all.

I believe this on most days, especially those days when blessed with a "sound mind," as Paul puts it to his young protégé, Timothy, just after the mentor reminds the fledgling pastor of the generational faith and trust exhibited by "your grandmother Lois and your mother Eunice" (2 Tim 1:5) and countless others whose acts of bravery and demeanor of centered peace shape any Christian life. There are other days (inevitably creating other states of mind) when storms seem to knock our sea legs out from under us, emotionally tearing us in half with fear and doubt.

Note how many times the Gospels refer to Jesus and the disciples traveling by water toward or from "the other side,"[19] a frantic crisscrossing of the Sea of Galilee in nautical trips that cumulatively suggest an intentional sacramental link between the disparate Jewish and gentile shores. In Mark, the two similar but separate feedings of thousands (6:30–42; 8:1–10) occur, interestingly, on opposite sides of the sea. The Gospel accounts invite the reader to notice water and how it forms and unites new followers of Jesus.

The twelve disciples often experience resistance (wind and storm) to such divinely authored mission trips (4:35–41) as Jesus leads his followers toward "the other" on yonder side, with isolated strangers (5:1) awaiting the crew as soon as they step out of the boat. It's worth noting several details of this particular storm before the sailors reach the beach. Fear attempts to interrupt the mission of gathered believers (the boat an early metaphor for Christ's church) in any era.[20]

"Leaving the crowd behind" (4:36), Jesus and his followers push off from the Jewish side of the sea. Jesus engages and cares about crowds in the Gospels, regularly interacting with them. There is consistently a clear distinction, however, between his public love for large groups of thirsty souls and private expectations of those who sign on as disciples. Unlike modern political leaders, always attempting to appease and pander to a supportive base, Jesus refuses to allow the reactions of the crowds to shape or define his mission and teaching. He listens to a voice whose origin resides in a kingdom not "from this world" (John 18:36), beyond the reach of any earthly threat or agenda-driven influence.

The thirteen men shove off, withdrawing, at night. Jesus boards the boat "just as he was." No flashy adornment, no carrot of reward or enticement, and really no explanation at all offered for the urgency of the night embarkation. "Other boats" are present, at least for a while. No one is excluded from obediently following the man into an eerie unknown.

Recalling Jonah's stormy (and also interrupted) mission to foreigners, the inevitable "windstorm"[21] arises (4:37), resulting in a swamped boat and a genuine fear of drowning—the very image adopted by the early church to express, liturgically, part of baptism's resultant power, circuitously realized in the next chapter in the drowning of swine.[22]

Jesus manages to sleep through the shouting and bailing, slumbering peacefully "on the cushion" (4:38). Here's part of a sermon I once preached on this text:

> I love the image of Jesus sleeping like a baby while the disciples run around the boat bailing for dear life. The story even describes a little pillow for the head of our Savior as water collects at the feet of his friends. It's almost comical. Can we get you anything else, Jesus? A glass of sherry? Maybe a little green-wrapped Andes mint for your pillow?
>
> Many years ago I had two teenagers, Peter and Andrew, in one of my hiking groups. They had a free-standing tent that required no stakes. The next morning, I got up early and noticed the boys had turned over in such a way that they were sleeping soundly on the roof of the tent; the floor straight up in the air. Some people can sleep through anything.
>
> The waves are crashing over the side of the boat. Mayhem among the crew running around. Early feelings of a first-century *Titanic*. And Jesus sleeps on. His disciples have to wake him up. And here, please note, is the very crux of the matter. The disciples have a question for Jesus when he wipes the sleep out of his eyes. This is also our question, if truth were told: "Teacher, do you not care that we are perishing?"[23]

Of course he cared, a rather loaded word used manipulatively in movies and television. "You don't care about me anymore, do you, John?" weeps an actress into the wind from a stormy cliff, confronting a lover. "And I'm coming to believe you *never* cared!"

Jesus "cares" about his friends. But his care here on the sea is similar to his concern revealed in the story of Lazarus. In Bethany, he raises his friend but centrally cares that the community is not jerked around by fear and the prospect of death. In the boat, he silences wind and wave, but there's much more at stake than an impressive nature miracle.

In the boat, Jesus "rebuked" (4:39) the wind rocking the swamped vessel, notably the same word used to silence the unclean spirit who tries to interrupt his ministry early in this same Gospel (1:25). Interestingly, the silencing of this unclean spirit—his first ministry encounter with evil in a public setting—occurs in a house of worship, not in some dark, shady locus "out there" promoted by populist politicians. Jesus is aware that even "good people" found in communities of faith (perhaps unknowingly) harbor false spirits intent upon derailing his teaching and central purpose.

Jesus silences the wind swamping the boat (read "church"), and "there [is] a dead calm" (4:39) on the water but a palpable lack of such on board. The silence in the boat could be sliced with a knife as Jesus looks around at his friends—each in turn, I'm guessing—before he finally speaks:

"Why are you afraid? Have you still no faith?" (4:40)

Please note: Jesus seems concerned here about the disciples' faith resources in the midst of a storm *much more than the storm itself*. It's a rather uppity pair of questions to pose to dripping-wet disciples barely afloat, lacking life preservers in water over their heads. Again, his emphatic interrogation after the storm is reminiscent of the confrontational tone he takes with the sisters and the crowd at the tomb of Lazarus. Death has no power over Jesus in either story. His primary concern in both tales is that his followers' *fear of death* maintains great and manipulative power, potentially paralyzing entire communities.

Predictably, the disciples (like me, much of the time) miss the nuance and still privately chat up the man's miracle of stilling wind and sea (4:41, "Wow, what an impressive guy!") rather than Jesus's centered and peaceful faith allowing him to sleep through storms and, in Bethany, arrive late for funerals.

I used to love the Mighty Mouse cartoons when I was a kid and ran around our yard in Chattanooga with a cape, singing the heroic theme song of the anthropomorphic rodent: *Here I Come to Save the Day!* Mighty Mouse always swooped in to save numerous days.

Jesus seems to swoop in many times in the Gospels. Note two observations, however, consistently bracketing how he "saves the day": (1) he's consistently telling disciples to be quiet about the miracle lest they misunderstand, or (2) he's offering a commentary on the miracle that seems to eclipse the relative importance of the miraculous event itself. Even more than stilling storms, Jesus is centrally concerned with forming disciples who can deal with storms in a nonanxious way.

Two chapters later in Mark, also at night, the disciples are again in a boat on the sea, this time without Jesus, who has climbed a mountain to pray alone (6:46). The wind on the water whips up. Jesus clearly sees their struggle, is completely aware of his friends' plight, and walks toward them with ambulatory buoyancy. I used to be utterly confused by this detail: "He intended to pass them by" (6:48). Why? First, he snoozes on the boat cushion through their frenzied fear before waking up and acting. Now he intends to seemingly ignore such fear altogether.

But doesn't this fit? Jesus is slowly forming disciples who will make up his church—disciples who will not so much have faith *in* Jesus but rather have the faith *of* Jesus. It's a subtle but critical distinction.

Jesus offers followers an amazing promise: "Anyone who hears my word and believes him who sent me *has* eternal life, and does not come under judgment, but has passed from death to life" (John 5:24). This is a radical present-tense identity capable of withstanding any darkness, any threat, any storm. Citing Daniel and his brave companions who stand up to lions, fire, and imprisonment in ancient stories of faith and bravery, Walter Brueggemann suggests such people "have an identity that is beyond the reach of the persecutor."[24] This is indeed the promise of baptism. We have already died in these ancient waters, now beyond the reach of any perceived threat to life.

George Yancy, professor of philosophy at Emory University in Atlanta, introduces themes of mortality and finitude early in each semester during class interactions with his students:

> To get them to think differently about our time together, to value our lives differently, I make a resolute effort to remind my students that all of us, at some point, sooner or later will become rotting corpses. That, I explain, is the great equalizer. . . . After hearing this, students will often become completely silent. . . . Yet a clarity emerges. My students and I see each other differently, perhaps for the very first time. We are no longer simply students and professor, but fragile creatures and mysterious beings who have been dying from the moment we were born in a universe with no self-evident ultimate meaning. Something as previously uneventful as sitting next to one's fellow classmate takes on unspeakable value. That shared understanding,

vulnerability, and mutual recognition of collective destiny makes our time together even more joyful, even more precious.[25]

In the same Gospel of Mark with the multiple sea crossings, Jesus, like a wise professor, attempts three times to stimulate discussion about his coming death and its honest details (8:31; 9:30–31; 10:32–34). After the first prediction, Peter throws a paternal arm around Jesus's shoulder, "[takes] him aside" (8:32), and offers a corrective rebuke-filled rejoinder, subsequently releasing Jesus's own tongue-lashing on the man. The second mortality prediction is followed by a collective community misunderstanding of his words, a description noting that the disciples are "afraid to ask him" (9:32) for clarification coupled with an amusing attempt to change the subject by arguing about their respective greatness. The third prediction is preceded by more fear (10:32) and followed by a comical request by James and John concerning celestial sycophancy. The nickname given by Jesus to these impetuous brothers (Boanerges, which means "Sons of Thunder"; 3:17) seems to fit here and sparks predictable anger from the other ten. In short, the disciples do not desire to talk about the imminent death of their leader (or, the reader presumes, death in general).

The disciples in Mark remind me of the Chinese relatives in the movie *The Farewell* (2019), who go to sometimes comical (but mostly sad) means of collaboration to protect their beloved Nai-Nai (Zhao Shuzhen in a powerful role) from the truth of her illness.[26] The movie centers upon a large, far-flung Asian family living in multiple countries coming together to face the mortality of a beloved matriarch, but the film also reveals dynamics potentially occurring in any family. "It's not the cancer that kills them," a daughter-in-law rationalizes for maintaining the pretense that all is well, "it's the fear." The movie slowly reveals who's really afraid. And it's not the one who's dying.

Fear will color and shape the narrative in Mark until the last verses of the book. In the most reliable endings of Mark, there are no comforting resurrection appearances and no calm post-death assurances from the risen Lord—only an angel at an empty tomb suggesting disciples can see Jesus in Galilee, "just as he told you" (16:7). Mark's Gospel account closes with female followers (the men have long since fled for the hills) hastily departing the tomb in silence and fear. With an elliptical invitation,[27] the curtain closes on this Gospel with the implication that Jesus can be found and realized in the very ministry encounters that began and characterized this Gospel in the sea crossings and various byways of Galilee. "Do you want to see Jesus?" the young man dressed in white at the empty tomb seems to ask. "Well, you just missed him. He's gone on ahead but will meet you in places and with people he's already introduced you to." Mark seems to imply that the story has the potential of beginning again.[28] Disciples have a clear choice: flee or follow.

"I want to know Christ," writes Saint Paul, "and the power of his resurrection and the sharing of his sufferings by becoming like him in his death" (Phil 3:10).

I desire and want a lot of things. Does the church really *want* what Paul wanted? The liturgical expression of such a desire is absolutely embedded in our sacrament of initiation into the community. "If any *want* to become my followers," Jesus clarifies after rebuking Peter's rebuke, "let them deny themselves and take up their cross and follow me" (Mark 8:34). There can be no arm-twisting here, no well-meaning evangelical coercion: *"If any want. . . ."*

Jesus is clear with those who do desire such a life. When the Lord calls people, Bonhoeffer told the church, "he bids them come and die."[29] We die with Christ in baptism, passing from death to life. Eternal life with the man begins, at any age, as we climb out of the water and dry off.

What prevents the church from desiring and living this radical promise instead of leaning on some bogus political source of salvation? Will we take Jesus "just as he [is]" (Mark 4:36) or rely on some other power to mightily swoop in and save us?

~~~~~~

One of the many gifts of the church year is that the Gospel story, cyclically retold from four vantage points, rubs the church's nose in death and mortality with an unbridled and persistent frequency whether the church likes it or not. Parishioners can, of course, refuse to pay attention and choose to dismiss the particulars of Holy Week, leaping each spring from Palm Sunday to Easter morning, entirely missing the power of the intervening events.[30] Even so, the church year regularly invites congregants to deal with a variety of texts that cannot be easily avoided unless a preacher chooses to opt out of the three-year lectionary altogether, relying instead upon a short list of Bible stories and themes that literally never rock the boat.

Jesus intends to disturb the boat that is the church for good reason: he is leading entire congregations toward adoption into a living reality punctuated by the inescapable fact that his followers have already died in baptism.

Essayist and fiction writer Brian Doyle (1956–2017) once wrote about a conversation he had with two anesthesiologists just before "going under" for a medical procedure. The conversation ranged between hobbies, children, and favorite music, but "what really got them going . . . was my question about what last remarks patients mumbled as the anesthetics took hold." Doyle writes,

> They told me that they'd noticed gender differences, for example that men would often joke until the very last second that they fell unconscious, probably as a defense against fear, while

women were often very concerned about being properly covered with the blankets until the last possible second. In my experience, said one anesthesiologist, children tend not to cry or whimper, but to just stare at me in abject terror and fearful trust. A child on the table always rattles me. Always. Many men and women, said the other anesthesiologist, murmur something at the end about how if they do not emerge from the operation safely, could we please tell their loved ones how much they were loved?[31]

"For the Spirit searches everything, even the depths of God" (1 Cor 2:10), Saint Paul writes to "the mature" (2:6) in the early church at Corinth. The word *everything* employed here to describe this stunningly broad search can seem rather daunting. Recalling Grover Crockett's "partial baptism" that opened this chapter, one can perhaps understand the old man's reluctance and inability to "take" the Holy Spirit's similar comprehensive intrusion into any of the multiple apprehensive fears that mark any of our lives.

"We speak of God's wisdom," Paul continues, "secret and hidden, which God decreed before the ages for our glory. None of the rulers of this age understood this; for if they had, they would not have crucified the Lord of glory" (2:7–8).

I sometimes wonder if the church should offer adult baptismal candidates (or, for child candidates, their parents and sponsors) an opportunity to voice any last words before "going under" the water to begin this wondrous new life, offering testimony to the strangeness of God's wisdom and power that fearful rulers of any age surely do not understand.

2

How Baptism Confronts Fear

I believe a great story told with power and love, a great poem or novel, a great wisdom text, a beautifully told and timely myth, a spontaneous cry from the heart, is not only the greatest force for change in humans, it is the only way . . . secret agents of the Unseen, unknown heroes and heroines, can penetrate the stupendous noise of the trillionfold Tower of Babel so innocently called "the internet" and speak to us.

—DAVID JAMES DUNCAN

In baptism, therefore, every Christian has enough to study and practice all his or her life. Christians always have enough to do to believe firmly what baptism promises and brings—victory over death and the devil, forgiveness of sin, God's grace, the entire Christ, and the Holy Spirit with his gifts. In short, the blessings of baptism are so boundless that if our timid nature considers them, it may well doubt whether they could all be true.

—MARTIN LUTHER, *THE LARGE CATECHISM* (1529)

If we live, we live to the Lord, and if we die,
we die to the Lord; so then, whether we live or
whether we die, we are the Lord's.

—ROMANS 14:8

In 1978, when my friend Edwin Sabuhoro was almost two, his
mother gathered her family, left most of their possessions behind,
and fled their African home to escape the maniacal reign of terror initiated by Idi Amin in Uganda—yet another nightmare for a
woman who'd already witnessed an enormous amount of suffering in
her homeland of Rwanda before leaving there. After a few days on
the run, Edwin's mother, Jolly, completely out of food and hope, with
enemies in pursuit, concluded that she could not face watching her
son starve to death, or worse. She reluctantly (and bravely) decided
to commit Edwin to the rapids of a river and the waiting arms of
God. Just before Jolly released her son into the depths, a United
Nations refugee vehicle appeared out of nowhere. They boarded the
van, which took them to temporary safety at a camp in Mbarara.

Forty years later, having overcome many incredible hardships and challenges, Edwin earned a doctorate in parks, rec-
reation, and tourism management from Clemson University
in South Carolina.[1] His special interest centers on preserving
mountain gorillas from poachers in Volcanoes National Park in
northwestern Rwanda (the same area where Dian Fossey once
worked), for which he won a CNN Hero Award in 2015.

David James Duncan (in the quote at the start of the chapter) is correct. Edwin's childhood encounter at the river remains
a primary narrative of great power for a man whose Christian
roots reside in the African Anglican tradition. "My mother was
so weak and had no milk for me," Edwin shared recently over a
meal. "She was going to throw me in the river because she could
not bear to watch me die so violently."

I left lunch that day with Edwin thinking of another old river that unites and fortifies God's people for any future challenge via our common dying and rising to new life in baptism. We have died (Rom 6), oddly thrown in the water by a loving parent and completely immersed in the grace of a whole new life. Blessed with this liquid identity, we are indeed "the Lord's," regardless of external threat, fortified by an ancient story with the power to liberate the church from any fear.

~~~~~~~

This chapter on baptism's power to confront fear commences with a brief examination of the early Christian community described in the book of Colossians. Acknowledging the debated authorship of this epistle, I'll employ Saint Paul's name in making a case for the sacramental identity the author shapes and calls forth throughout the letter.

Colossae, located in the valley of the Lycus River (modern-day Turkey), was a "relatively small town"[2] when Paul penned this letter from prison. "Remember my chains," he implores in the last verse of the letter. The time of writing is unclear, but many think the letter coincides with Paul's two-year house arrest in Rome described in the final verses of the book of Acts.

The congregation may have been organized by Paul's friend Epaphras, mentioned twice in Colossians as one who schooled the community in the grace of God (1:6–7) and was pastorally "always wrestling" in prayer (4:12) on behalf of the congregation, even while away from his friends. Epaphras is also mentioned at the close of the book of Philemon, establishing a connection to Onesimus, a Colossian and the runaway slave who hand-delivers (with Tychicus) Paul's letter (4:9) to Colossae. It's possible that Epaphras first encountered Paul from the evangelist's sermons and teaching stint in Ephesus (about one hundred miles away) and excitedly brought the word of grace back to his small town, gathering a group of believers that became an early Christian community.

Paul, then, from a distance, addresses this congregation in writing as an esteemed authority who's never actually visited their little town in the flesh. It's rather daring to remind relative strangers, the saints in Colossae, how they've been "buried with [Christ] in baptism" (2:12) and have already "died to the elemental spirits of the universe" (2:20) before drawing their last breaths. "For you have died," the relentless man drives home a third time, "and your life is hidden with Christ in God" (3:3). As I make a case for their place as a thesis for this book, it's important to examine these three statements in the wider context of Paul's letter to discover how the diminutive tentmaker was able to pull off declaring such powerful sacramental truths without causing the Colossians to run (with old Grover Crockett) for the Turkish hills. The sources of fear were admittedly different in the first century than now. The trenchant grip of the threat of death, however, is similar in any century, often luring parishioners to adopt beliefs and practices that have little to do with inherited tradition. Luther's words from "A Sermon on Preparing to Die" (1519) speak to any era:

> Death looms so large and is terrifying because our foolish and fainthearted nature has etched its image too vividly within itself and constantly fixes its gaze on it. Moreover, the devil presses man to look closely at the gruesome mien and image of death to add to his worry, timidity, and despair. Indeed, he conjures up before man's eyes all the kinds of sudden and terrible death ever seen, heard, or read by man . . . so that burdened with such thoughts man forgets God, flees and abhors death, and thus, in the end, is and remains disobedient to God.[3]

Paul, like Luther, is concerned that false and lax teaching might result in a spiritually anemic church. Early in the letter, he writes, "I want you to know how much I am struggling for you, and for those in Laodicea, and for all who have not seen me face to face" (Col 2:1). Laodicea was a neighboring town just up the road from Colossae, less than ten miles away. The crucified and risen Christ tragically addresses these same Laodiceans in the book of Revelation not many decades later: "I know your works; you are neither cold nor hot." *I frankly wish you were one or the other*, he seems to say. "So, because you are lukewarm, and neither cold nor hot, I am about to spit you out of my mouth" (Rev 3:15–16).

It's a rather graphic image, this spitting-and-rejecting Jesus, perhaps one of the most pointed and devastating things our Lord ever said. He apparently prefers completely indifferent and skeptical folk over those who occasionally dabble in the faith, lukewarm at best. (I'd also add that the former are often a lot more interesting.[4]) Paul is rather prescient here with the Laodiceans. If the neighbors just up the road eventually lapse into a *meh*-state of lukewarmth, his worry for these Colossians is well-founded.

Paul's many imperative instructions in the letter are meant to counter a Christianity that (he's observed) sometimes never matures—"put to death" (3:5); "get rid of" (3:8); "clothe yourselves" (3:14); "let the word of Christ dwell" (3:16); "sing psalms, hymns" (3:16); "devote yourselves to prayer" (4:2); "let your speech always be gracious, seasoned with salt" (4:6). All these imperative verbs may make legalistically wary Lutherans a bit nervous, but they're offered as advice for people who've *already died* and are intended to further form disciples with spiritual depth that any grave cultural threat would be unable to touch. Disciplines strengthen disciples.

Please notice that Paul does not begin with the imperative. Indicative baptismal observations come first: You were buried (2:12). You have died (3:3). Paul's imperatives that follow are not a list of rigid legalisms but rather spiritual CPR for dead and buried baptized people. Compassion, kindness, humility, meekness, and patience (3:12) are not merit badge achievements; they are instead the very breath of God conveyed to the baptized by the Spirit. "Clothe yourselves," says Paul, with these gifts, baptismal garments for a new spiritual wardrobe. The verb here, again, undoubtedly shaped early sacramental garbing practices immediately following a candidate's watery welcome, "no doubt stamping upon the consciousness of the newly baptized and the community as a whole," writes Ron Byars, "the fact that baptism was meant to be a movement from one identity to another,"[5] a practice laden with much more meaning than our latter-day donning of an inherited baptismal garment (albeit a touching tradition) that may have been used in the same family for generations.

Every imperative verb used by Paul to encourage the Colossians should be read in light of people who have died and are buried in baptism, rising to a new way of life. These are not legalisms. Paul is instead describing communal drowning in Jesus and disciples now breathing God's new air—traveling gifts for the newly born.

Similarly, Romans 6:1–11 and its multiple references to dying with Christ through baptism function in a related strategic way for Paul when he reaches the ethical section of the book in Romans 12. Here he employs the almost-thunderous "therefore" (12:1) in reference to his entire preceding theological argument, suggesting that a baptized person's very death in Christ therefore allows such a raised community to "present [their] bodies as a living sacrifice" (12:1) and engage in a variety of new behaviors that are not, collectively, some fiery sermon filled with imperative scolding but rather core spiritual characteristics of people who've already died and are now able to offer a contrasting way of life to neighbors in their place of residence: "let love be genuine" (12:9), "contribute to the needs of the saints" (12:13), "bless those who persecute you" (12:14), and "live peaceably with all" (12:18), to mention just four of several resurrection traits Paul lists after his lengthy eleven-chapter theological précis.

Central in Paul's baptismal letter to the Colossians from his place of confinement is a bold description of the lengthening and widening of God's agenda in the world, sometimes perceived by Christians to cover concerns of a fairly limited nature—family, country, and congregation. If it's true that in baptism God has "rescued us from the power of darkness and transferred us into the kingdom of his beloved Son" (Col 1:13), then the rescue and transference (now, in the present, in this life) suggest a broad citizenship and theological purview for "[Christ's] body—that is, the church" (1:24) that Paul wastes little time in describing.

In the intervening verses between the last two scripture citations, much of which is thought to be an early Christian hymn, Paul repeats the phrase *all things* at least five times. My usual afternoon news program is *All Things Considered* on National Public Radio. The Christ whom Paul reveals and praises in Colossians has been airing a similarly titled theological program for countless millennia. If this section of Colossians (1:15–20) is indeed an early hymn, it's not difficult to detect the refrain and how it shows up multiple centuries later in the second verse of one of my favorite hymns: "Praise to the Lord, who o'er all things is wondrously reigning."[6]

The breadth of the Christological agenda here is nothing short of immense. "All things in heaven and on earth were created" (1:16) through Christ, whether visible or hidden—easily covering galaxies, giraffes, goldfish, and the gamma ray. Christ is "before all things, and in him all things hold together" (1:17), a statement that completely reshapes my rather pedestrian prayer life every time I come upon it, not to mention my ideas concerning "all the fullness of God" (1:19), who seems "pleased to dwell" in this same Christ. My narrow understanding of Christ's redemptive scope is widened as the breathtaking reconciliation of "all things, whether on earth or in heaven" (1:20) through the blood of his cross really hits home—not just with my favorite and nearby humans. *All things.* It almost goes without saying that this Christ will "have first place in everything" (1:18), but my own confession, even as a pastor for over three decades, is that he often doesn't. Someone once aptly said, "Don't try slapping God on the back; you'll miss." God's agenda for the cosmos will not be domesticated for my own purposes and biases.

If Paul's letter to these Colossians includes ethical remind-ers (chapters 3 and 4) *following* radical statements that the baptized have died in Christ and are now capable of living in such a risky way, this dramatic and broad hymn-like agenda (chapter 1) *at the onset* of his correspondence surely gives the passionate inmate's prison pen the courage to state such a dar-ing sacramental truth out loud—you were buried; you've died. "I have been crucified with Christ," Paul says elsewhere, "and it is no longer I who live, but it is Christ who lives in me" (Gal 2:19–20). Factoring in Paul's Colossian claims, dying with Christ cannot authentically result in some tepid Laodicean life. Gordon T. Smith writes,

> Baptism itself is a political act as much as it is a moral act. Through baptism we declare that our ultimate allegiance is not to family of origin, tribe, or nation, but to Christ; indeed, baptism is an act of defiance against any human authority— family or culture or nation—that would in any way, shape, or form compete with or undermine our loyalty to Christ. . . . Just as a ring for a married person is a continual reminder of their covenant identity, commitments, and the joy of married love, so also for the Christian, water becomes a reminder of the wonder of their union with Christ.[7]

The letter to the Colossians reveals one man's passion for a wide agenda for Christ's church that's radically in concert with God's. Not even prison's depressing confinement could temper that passion. It's a dangerous letter for the church to read in any age because it explodes any attempt to retain the status quo with a partisan nationalism that borders upon idolatry.

~~~~~~

What difference would it make if an entire congregation truly believed they'd already died in baptism, according to Paul's Colossian convictions, and were now swimming around in the grace of God on this side of their last breaths? How would such sacramental conviction change how a Christian community lived in the world, shared their resources, and interacted with one another in love? Can a return to our baptismal roots form a congregation that's not necessarily heedless of external threat but certainly not paralyzed by or overly fearful of such?

"There's a lot out there that can grab any of us at any time," a worried parishioner once told me. And she's right.

On my front steps one Monday afternoon in Walhalla, South Carolina, I squinted to bring the small print into focus while reading the instructions on a package of Predator plastic earthworms. Moles were ravaging our front yard that summer. The bait craftily resembled their preferred subterranean diet, laced with just enough poison to do the trick. The package featured an angry-looking black cat on the cover, ready to pounce. I preferred that afternoon not to think of the lawn pests as something with gender and a daily life, despite singing "All Things Bright and Beautiful" with great gusto not many Sundays before in church—"all creatures great and small," posited the peppy refrain.

"With your bare finger," the Predator instructions read, "carefully locate the interior of the mole tunnel (about an inch in diameter) while disturbing as little soil as possible. Slowly thread at least half of the plastic worm along the tunnel floor."

I easily located the tunnel and felt in both directions, marveling at the circular symmetry and precision (amazing work, Mr. Mole), and offered a final finger-wiggle to make sure I had enough room to thread in the poisonous bait.

My wife, Cindy, arrived on the front porch from the kitchen, wide-eyed in response to my loud scream. Her husband held aloft a wildly shaking right hand.

"That damn thing just grabbed me with its flippers!"

It didn't really hurt, just scared me momentarily, like some unseen and unexpected force jumping out of the shadows in a horror movie. A yard-obsessed gardener doesn't anticipate getting grabbed like that, under the earth, out of the blue.

All pastors, however, have to deal with lots of invisible forces resulting in lasting damage much graver than mole tunnels. A congregation is grabbed by many things year in and out that shake our convictions and make us collectively cautious and afraid. I write these words inside a quiet house, "socially distanced" during the coronavirus pandemic with our church building two miles away shuttered for many Sundays. How will a little water and a few ancient words make much of a difference in a world with so many things lurking in the shadows to grab us and bring us down?

In late May of 2018, a year and a half after retirement and a couple months after my dad's death, an old friend, Larry (a Legal Aid attorney), and I boarded loaded bicycles for a long forty-two hundred-mile trip across the northern tier of the country. With the blessing of understanding wives, we dipped rear wheels in the waters of Puget Sound at Anacortes, Washington, and headed east toward the Maine coast, a journey that would cross three mountain ranges (Cascades, Rockies, and Adirondacks) and last seventy-seven days through all sorts of weather, including a driving snow at the top of a high mountain pass. We often camped along the way in parks and out of sight in the woods and met lots of interesting people who were surprisingly forthcoming with two strangers, sharing opinions about regional and national politics, faith and doubt, and life in small towns and several cities. Our bicycle route crossed the wide expanse of rural Montana and North Dakota but also passed through urban areas, including Fargo, Minneapolis, Cleveland, and Buffalo.

Larry and I rode into the small town of Wenona, Illinois, late one afternoon in mid-July, looking for the town park we'd heard about with a free shower for touring cyclists. A hospitable and very welcoming resident named Matt led us in his truck to the park about three blocks off Main Street. He worked throughout the county as a first responder. We talked for a good while before setting up tents. Matt described the location of the best diner in town, and we shared a few details about our respective vocations—a pastor, an attorney, and an EMT.

The three of us sat in the last light of the day and spoke of family and home. Matt told us about the challenges of his work. It was getting dark; no one seemed to care. Even though we hailed from very different parts of the country, we had a lot in common, sitting across from each other on two park benches as the sun went down.

"This is about the time of day three Julys ago, right after dusk with car headlights coming on, when I got a call at home about a bad wreck on the main highway about three miles out of town." Matt paused for half a minute while we listened to a chorus of crickets. "I arrived at the scene and saw a vehicle that looked a little in the dark like my son's old Impala. It was overturned in a ditch. I was the first medical person there. The driver had been thrown clear out of the car near the boundary of the cornfield, face down, not moving." Matt paused again. "It was him, my son, hardly a scratch. He was gone, just like that."

Larry and I headed east out of town the next morning, pedaling toward Indiana, roughly two days from Wenona. I thought of Matt for several days as we rode, praying for him. I think of him still. I often wonder how people like Matt live with such agonizing and horrible events. What difference indeed can baptism make with people who are grabbed and gripped by such suffering?

~~~~~

In his wonderful collection of linked short stories, *Strangers to Temptation*, Scott Gould describes coming of age in Kingstree, a small town in the South Carolina Lowcountry. The narrator, recalling life at thirteen, confesses to his mother one Saturday afternoon that he's worried about dying, especially since his best friend, Lonnie, jumped off the river bridge for a summer swim and lost an eye from an encounter with an abandoned and submerged Kenmore refrigerator:

> "Get used to it," she said, fanning herself with a dishtowel. For a nurse, she could be pretty harsh inside her own house. "Listen, I got enough worrying all to myself. That's what church is for. Church is where you go to clear your head. So you just keep sitting there beside me and listen to [Reverend] Scoggins and one day a switch will flip on and you'll get about half of life figured out. The other half will stay a mystery. Half is about the best you can hope for."[8]

I'd probably never be quite so direct with a child, but perhaps she's got the percentage about right. "Look," Peter once said rather sassily to Jesus, "we have left everything and followed you" (Matt 19:27). It's coming clear to this disciple that Jesus's teachings about life (in this case, concerning wealth and possessions and their relationship to salvation) won't make complete and immediate sense at first. Pay close attention to the places in the Gospels where brassy disciples talk back to the Lord. They're usually reflecting our own misgivings and doubts out loud, trying to figure out their own percentage of life.

I'll never forget a conversation I once had with someone who wanted to hear from a more active and transparent God. "I've prayed," she said. "I pray all the time. I ask God for guidance and strength. But what I'd really like is for God to speak to me. Just once. Why doesn't God talk to us, Pastor Frank? I know God speaks through the Bible and through others. But out loud, I mean. Unmistakably, so I can hear him and truly believe he's there. Has God ever spoken to you? Out loud? I'm sure he has or you wouldn't be doing what you're doing. So why hasn't he spoken to me? I pray and pray and all I really hear is silence. I feel like I'm talking to myself after all these years. Would it be so hard for him to speak to me? Just a sentence or two would help. I don't think that's asking so much."

We talked for quite a while that afternoon. I admitted that God had never spoken to me out loud either, at least not in a disembodied voice. That maybe God has our best interests in mind by *not* speaking out loud, shielding us from the inevitable raised eyebrow upon reporting to a friend that we've just heard such a voice.

The Old Testament, of course, reports many instances of a rather loquacious God—one who speaks in ancient gardens, from within a burning bush, while transcribing tablets of instruction, upon confronting wayward kings, firing up the prophets. In Joseph Heller's wickedly funny novel *God Knows*, King David describes his chatty relationship with God prior to the Bathsheba incident:

> I inquired for guidance whenever I wished to. He could always
> be counted on to respond. Our talks were sociable and precise.

No words were wasted. "Should I go down to Keilah and save the city?" I asked while still a fugitive in Judah. "Go down to Keilah and save the city," He answered helpfully. "Should I go up to Hebron in Judah and allow the elders to crown me king?" I asked after receiving news of Saul's death and completing my famous elegy. "Why not?" God obliged me in reply.[9]

God talks out loud a lot in the Hebrew Bible, with a variety of central characters, but is fairly restrained after that. "Very few people," writes Barbara Brown Taylor, "come to see me because they want to discuss something God said to them last night. The large majority come because they cannot get God to say anything at all."[10] So maybe it behooves the church to pay special attention to those rare occurrences when God does speak in the New Testament, like at Jesus's baptism in the waters of an old river (Matt 3:13–17).

Jesus shows up at the river and gets in line beside sinners. This confuses John the Baptist a bit (3:14), but Jesus will consistently rub shoulders with sinners throughout his ministry. Down into the water he goes, and then comes the voice, rare in the New Testament, "This is my Son, the Beloved, with whom I am well pleased" (3:17). Not much is said here. But it's important not to miss what God does say: three incredible things.

1. *Jesus is God's child.* This is certainly God's declaration for Jesus but also the church's theological claim at every baptism: "We are born children of a fallen humanity; by water and the Holy Spirit we are reborn children of God and made members of the church, the body of Christ."[11] I was indeed born a son of Ruth and Bob Honeycutt on May 15, 1957. I will always be one of their three sons. But I was reborn a child of God on July 28 of that same year in downtown Chattanooga, among the saints at Ascension

Lutheran. My primary identity is as a child of God. It's interesting that Jesus does nothing of note in the Gospels until after his baptism. His remarkable ministry seems to be utterly grounded in his empowering identity as God's child. Ditto for the church.

2. *Jesus is greatly loved, the beloved.* This is also the church's proclamation anytime baptism is celebrated. One could accurately refer to baptism as "liquid love"—God's declaration that this love will never be withdrawn, a powerful message in a world of conditional "if . . . then" assertions. God may not always be pleased with human behavior, but divine love is never retracted or offered with a contingency clause.

Fifteen years ago, I met a man named Robert on death row in the lower part of our state who sincerely desired to die for committing a horrible crime that occurred while he was off medication prescribed for schizophrenia. The guilt associated with the incident, an act he could not even remember, was understandably overwhelming with clear evidence of wrongdoing. Robert and I developed an ongoing relationship with visits and letters that have continued to this day. Lots of events have occurred since our first meeting, including the caring guidance of a defense team that worked with the victim's family and the South Carolina judicial system to ultimately arrange a plea agreement for life in prison for Robert with no hope of parole. Today, Robert teaches a Bible study in his prison and leads a program that helps new inmates beginning a sentence. I'm convinced that his turnaround and purpose for living has come about through several on his defense team reminding him repeatedly of an identity that began long ago in the font of his childhood church with a God who gives up on no one.

3. *Jesus pleases God and brings the Creator great delight.* In the various Gospel narratives describing his baptism, Jesus has

done nothing to date that seems to warrant such pleasure, at least not in the way it's usually measured and awarded in the world's economy. God simply delights in his child and says so. As a young father, I caught myself in the role of "correctional officer" far too often, pointing out the mistakes and foibles in my children. It's easy to do this as a parent. And it's easy to forget how important it is to say how very pleased we are with them. I led a children's sermon once and invited moms and dads to accompany their kids forward to the altar. After briefly describing the scene at Jesus's baptism, I asked the parents to think of something that truly pleased them about their child and whisper that very thing in their child's ear. The tender and surprised reaction of the children was the real message that day. God speaks sheer and unconditional delight to his Son and to his latter-day children. The church is called to pass along this pleasure to others.

I'll never forget that conversation in my office: "Why is God so silent?" she asked. "Could God not speak to me? Just once?"

I wish I'd thought to tell her the three things spoken at Jesus's baptism day are still spoken out loud to her and everyone welcomed into his body with water and word. It's not a bad place to start for anyone fearful of death, trying to make sense of their own percentage of this life.

~~~~~~

We moved an insanely heavy stone baptismal font once.

For close to nine years in midcareer, I served an inner-city congregation in Columbia, South Carolina, that gathered for worship in a beautiful neo-Gothic sanctuary built in 1930. The original on-site church building was burned by General Sherman at the end of the Civil War. John Bachman (1790–1874), a Lutheran pastor and naturalist, hid several paintings, sketches, and an abundance of notes originating with his good friend, John James Audubon (1785–1851), in the basement of the original building at the onset of the war. Bachman was sure they'd be safe in the central part of the state away from Charleston. The amount of lost Audubon material, I'm told, was substantial.

The present Ebenezer sanctuary is stunningly beautiful and remains a "destination church" for people who admire church architecture. The nearby Lutheran seminary uses Ebenezer for the spring graduation service. The movie *Nailed* (rereleased as *Accidental Love*), starring Jake Gyllenhaal and Jessica Biel, borrowed the chancel and nave for a wedding scene. A high pulpit, long center aisle, elevated altar on the east wall, and cruciform seating arrangement all suggest tradition, permanence, and respect for liturgical order. Not a lot has changed in the space for many decades.

Many Lutheran churches possess tiny baptismal fonts that may visually undermine the largesse of God during the celebration of the sacrament. The challenge with Ebenezer's baptistery was not size. The space itself was ample. The stone font held a copious amount of water when full. The sight lines, however, from most seats in the nave to a baptism's dramatic action were quite poor. We decided to appoint a study committee and investigate the possibility of moving the font to a more central location.

The ten-person committee met monthly for close to a year. Comprised of members of various ages and congregational longevity, the group spent plenty of time together and studied baptism from many biblical and theological angles. Different writers from the committee published articles in the church newsletter. We invited the congregation to a series of small-group discussions. One member of the group, George, in his late eighties, who jokingly told me he'd "been a member of Ebenezer since before the Punic Wars," was originally opposed to moving the font to the center aisle. During the congregational meeting where we voted on the proposed change, George stood and made an impassioned speech about baptism, unrehearsed and unprompted—what it meant to him, how his mind had changed, and why. "If we've already died in this ancient gift of welcome into Christ's body, alive in his grace," he said, "shouldn't we move our font to a more central place to remind us who we are as we walk to the altar for communion?" George, widely respected in the church and community, brought a couple people to tears. It was a moving speech. The vote passed handily.

We consulted structural engineers who crawled below the sanctuary to examine weight-bearing beams. The font weighed at least a thousand pounds. It had to be cut into two pieces and gingerly moved by several strapping guys recruited by the engineering company. My colleague, Paul, still kids me and wonders "whether [I] conveniently scheduled to be out of town for 'a meeting' the day we sliced through the base and moved the whole operation with a lot of prayer."

Today, my tenure at Ebenezer long concluded, the font in the center aisle looks like it's always been there, just before the steps into the chancel. Worshippers pause, dip their hands, and trace a moist cross on their foreheads before receiving Christ's body and blood. We welcomed homeless people to worship at Ebenezer. A daily evening meal was served for many months until the ministry outgrew our building and was taken over by the Salvation Army. One homeless man, unsure exactly what to do as he came forward alongside the water one Sunday morning, immersed his entire bearded face and came up dripping, beaming—an appropriate response, I thought.

"For as often as you eat this bread and drink the cup, you proclaim the Lord's death until he comes" (1 Cor 11:26). Such an oddly liberating proclamation is now undeniably assisted by the font's central location, with Saint Paul's provocative assertion recalled by even the very young: "We have been buried with him by baptism into death, so that, just as Christ was raised from the dead by the glory of the Father, so we too might walk in newness of life" (Rom 6:4).

Immediately following Jesus's baptism in all three synoptic accounts, he journeys into the wilderness for an encounter with the devil, who tempts him not with things that look all that bad but with things that look quite good[12]—to be pertinent, sensational, and omnipotent. Baptism apparently does not protect us from such tempting encounters. In fact, biblically speaking, the sacrament may heighten and hasten such. With Christ, however, we the baptized have died. Temptation does not have the same twisted allure. Baptism promotes trust, relinquishment, and sacrifice in the face of temptation. Fear not.

In her poem "Coffins," Faith Shearin describes how people were once very afraid of being buried alive and waking up subterranean. Some coffins were equipped with axes, shovels, and even trumpets, others with spring-tripped lids that would pop open if a body "shifted in the depths of that eternal rest."[13]

My grandmother, who grew up in Bainbridge, Georgia, used to tell enraptured grandchildren about a wealthy woman in her town, fearful of burial, whose body was laid to rest aboveground with a glass top on the coffin. "She wanted to still feel the morning sun," Grandmother said. Teenagers would sneak out to the woman's far pasture on her farm with candles, climb the stone funeral cairn, and look down at her through the glass to see if her hair and fingernails had grown longer. The local police finally had to put a stop to it all and she was buried.

The movie To Dust (2018) brings together a Hasidic cantor, Shmuel (played by the wonderful Geza Rohrig), and a biology professor from a local community college named Albert (played by the amusing Matthew Broderick). The pair forms an unlikely partnership. Shmuel increasingly worries about his deceased wife's body, specifically the rate of her body's decomposition under the earth. He enlists the good professor to help him find out. They run tests in Albert's lab with several soil types. Nothing seems to bring Shmuel any peace as it increasingly dawns on him how fast his wife's body is returning to dust. The movie sounds darkly morbid. Rohrig and Broderick, however, bring an unusual acting chemistry to many tender, poignant, and even funny moments. I came away pondering how difficult it would be to let go of my own wife of forty years if she were to precede me to the grave but also took great comfort in the church's annual Lenten reminder, an ashen cross recalling baptism, that we're all created from dust (Gen 3:19) and will eventually return there.

We spent our third year of marriage in the mountains of Watauga County, North Carolina, for my seminary internship shared by two congregations. The smaller of the two, Holy Communion Lutheran, is located at an elevation of over four thousand feet, the highest of any ELCA church building east of the Rockies. I'm still intrigued by their funeral policy that did not allow backhoes in the church cemetery. All the graves were dug by hand by able-bodied church members who gathered for a labor of love that took most of the day. Stories were told and grief was shared as tools were passed around. I recall being over my head in a grave one Saturday afternoon with a pickax, thinking what a strange but powerful lesson I was learning.

The first three illustrations listed above—burial phobias, fear of darkness, and obsession with mortality—reflect various trepidations most people consider from time to time. The fourth illustration—the church immersed in a series of graves while sharing stories of life and hope—suggests the importance of a vigorous baptismal catechesis within congregational life that slowly shapes courage, bravery, and nerve capable of facing any fear.

We all "walk through the valley of the shadow of death" (Ps 23:4 NKJV). The *shadow* that death casts over life creates a long valley of fear and worry often worse than death itself, prompting hasty prayers of rescue and protection. It's through this valley that the church undeniably walks. "Every second," writes novelist Anthony Doerr, "a million petitions wing past the ear of God."

> Let it be door number two. Get Janet through this. Make Mom fall in love again, make the pain go away, make this key fit. If I fish this cove, plant this field, step into this darkness, give me the strength to see it through. Help my marriage, my sister, me. What will this fund be worth in thirteen days? In thirteen years? Will I be around in thirteen years? And the most unanswerable of unanswerables: Don't let me die.[14]

"Surely goodness and mercy shall follow me all the days of my life" (Ps 23:6). The Hebrew word for "follow" in the psalm, *radaph*, is a much more aggressive verb than one might think at first glance. The same word is used to describe Pharaoh and his chariots that hastily pursue the children of God toward the Red Sea. The man intends to catch those who flee toward the water. "Follow" in this famous psalm is not a slow amble, lagging somewhere behind in the far distance. "Goodness and mercy" hastily tail and chase down God's people all the days of our lives with divine intent. God follows; God intends to catch us.

"Fear not," therefore, is indeed an appropriate refrain of comfort in both testaments. Perfect love (God's goodness and mercy constantly in pursuit) drives out any fear (1 John 4:18) or future apprehension.

How might the church, those who "dwell in the house of the Lord," embrace the powerful promises of baptism in ways that demote death's fearful grip on a congregation, offering prayers of trust that need not sound frantic? Like it or not, pastors must take the lead in this regard. Every flock needs a leader called by the Great and Good Shepherd who fearlessly announces our sacramental death in the waters, now raised to a new life.

He has rescued us from the power of darkness and transferred us into the kingdom of his beloved Son. (Col 1:13)

When you were buried with him in baptism, you were also raised with him through faith in the power of God. (Col 2:12)

So if you have been raised with Christ, seek the things that are above, where Christ is, at the right hand of God. (Col 3:1)

For you have died, and your life is hidden with Christ in God. (Col 3:3)

We've died. Past tense.

Pastoral proclamation in the present is largely creative commentary on what's already occurred.

3

The Role of Preaching and Pastoral Care in Forming Sacramental Identity

~~~~~~

A preacher needs to be a sage in order to speak responsibly from the pulpit each week. She has to have something worth listening to on some of the mightiest subjects in the world, including how the universe looks to a Christian, who human beings are, the human predicament, God's gracious address to the predicament in Jesus Christ, the resulting prognosis for our world, and, along the way, much, much else. . . . The preacher has to be a little crazy to tackle all this. Or else, like the Apostle Paul, she needs to have seen the risen Lord.

—Cornelius Plantinga Jr.

I do a deal, a great deal of my work in churches, usually during the homily, when all but the most besotted acolytes are in a state of surreal boredom verging on hallucination.

—Glen Duncan, Satan in *I, Lucifer*

A good sermon is never a neat package tied up with a bow. Rather, a good sermon is like rings

on the surface of a lake where a swimmer has
gone down in deep water.

—Edmund Steimle

In his powerful book about his family's generational funeral
home business in Milford, a small Michigan community,
Thomas Lynch describes a horrible accident that occurred one
night while he was on call.[1] A Roman Catholic family from Milford was traveling toward Georgia along the interstate in their
van. The parents rode up front. A daughter, Stephanie (named
for Saint Stephen, the martyr), slept in the middle seat. Three
other children cuddled in the back.

As they drove through Kentucky after midnight, some local
boys were busy tipping headstones in a cemetery. The boys
stole one of the stones, weighing fourteen pounds, but soon
grew tired of carrying it. "With not so much malice as mis-
chief," according to Lynch, the boys dropped the stone from
the bridge spanning the nearby interstate. The stone descended
through darkness, intersected with the windshield of the van
from Michigan (traveling at seventy miles per hour) just as the
vehicle reached the bridge, glanced off the father's shoulder, and
struck Stephanie in the chest as she slept in the middle seat.
She did not die instantly. A trucker stopped as they all waited
for an ambulance in the dark rural early morning, reciting the
rosary. Stephanie died two hours later in the local hospital from
a broken sternum and irreparably bruised heart.

Lynch, also a poet, offers several poignant observations on
the senseless tragedy. But I read the story and was left wondering: *What will the preacher say at this funeral? How will this
family's pastor minister to them and the congregation in the coming
weeks?*

Forming a congregation around the biblical truth that followers of Christ have already died in baptism before they breathe their last will require a thoughtful long-term preaching strategy from even the most skilled pastors. Part of the reason so many statements of questionable assistance pepper a time of tragedy ("She's gone to a better place where God needed her," etc.) is that many Christians have not been formed with a mature vocabulary of baptism and the sacrament's liberating lexicon of life. Addressing pastors, Robert Hughes notes, "No longer can we assume that our congregation knows the tradition of its denomination . . . something like a doctrinal defoliation has occurred."[2]

Baptism does not instantly and inherently soften the blow of intense grief. Perhaps the best initial response with a deeply grieving person may be something akin to the caring communal reaction of Job's friends, who, after his tragedy, "sat with him on the ground seven days and seven nights, and no one spoke a word to him, for they saw that his suffering was very great" (Job 2:13). Job's pals flunk their subsequent attempts at pastoral care in the chapters that follow, but I think they got it right there at first. Grief requires silent accompaniment and shared anguish rather than quick explanation.

But mature Christian formation—brought along and assisted in a fashion resembling spiritual midwifery via any authentic preaching ministry—surely facilitates healing in community over time and offers a theological perspective with a longer view eclipsing trite greeting card bromides, one acute danger often filling a spiritual void, posttragedy, born through a congregation fed a regular diet of easy answers.

In the following pages, I want to offer several observations about the role of preaching in helping to shape and form Christian communities capable of reflecting, baptismally, upon the tragic acts that end the lives of people like Stephanie on a dark Kentucky interstate.

Tell the Truth

Neal Plantinga is spot-on when he says "the preacher has to be a little crazy" to tackle such a wide variety of theological topics raised in Scripture as they intersect with the questions parishioners bring to worship weekly and ponder privately, if not out loud, with only a few trusted friends.[3] There is much more doubt and skepticism in the hearts and minds of even the most committed churchgoers than many pastors are sometimes willing to admit.

In addition to the well-known skepticism of Saint Thomas, whose courage to express doubt eventually leads to the most mature Christological confession in that Gospel (John 20:28, "My Lord and my God!"), all three Synoptic Gospels include honest Easter narrative details suggesting that the disciples' excitement is also faithfully colored with intellectual and emotional restraint—"While in their joy they were disbelieving and still wondering" (Luke 24:41), "When they saw him, they worshiped him; but some doubted" (Matt 28:17), "They said nothing to anyone because they were afraid" (Mark 16:8). Embracing these scriptural cues, it is therefore vitally important for the preacher to be honest about his or her own faith struggles and avoid the type of proclamation that always seems to tidily wrap up the sermon with a nice nonthreatening bow each Sunday.

Faithful sermons will regularly reveal how the preacher doesn't have it all figured out this side of the grave. After teaching confirmation classes for three decades, I've noticed that savvy youth can especially serve as allies for the preacher. Teenagers, many equipped with expansive BS detectors, will often say aloud what their parents (and other adults) may choose to keep cloaked. Tick Roby, a gifted art student at the local Maine high school in Richard Russo's novel *Empire Falls*, reminds me of several young people of my acquaintance who've served as valuable homiletical companions in helping to shape authentic sermons:

> Tick's strategy for dealing with lying adults is to say nothing and watch the lies swell and constrict in their throats. When this happens, the lie takes on a physical life of its own and must be either expelled or swallowed. Most adults prefer to expel untruths with little burplike coughs behind their hands, while others chuckle or snort or make barking sounds. . . . By their very nature, Tick suspects, lies seek open air. They don't like being confined in dark, cramped places.[4]

Preachers like me may not intentionally lie in a sermon. But it's always helpful to imagine someone like Tick among your listeners, waiting to see if your pulpit efforts may be accompanied by the equivalent of "burplike coughs" or downright truth-masking "barking sounds."

The congregations I served all had three-year confirmation programs. Usually, one of those years (the other two focused upon *The Small Catechism* and companion units on the Old and New Testaments) was spent building a candid list of questions developed by students. Their questions, tackled one by one, served to shape the curriculum for that school year. Our reflections (without calling attention to the source) often made their way into sermons as the breadth of the lectionary cycle unfolded. Any question was fair game ranging from the serious ("Who created God?") to the whimsical ("If Jesus had played golf in Galilee, what would have been his favorite club and why?"). We noted the limit of our understanding "in a mirror, dimly"[5] and "only in part" (1 Cor 13:12). We consulted ancient texts related to their questions, brought in specialists in certain fields, and watched clips from movies like the following from Woody Allen's *Love and Death* (1975), where Boris, a Russian pacifist soldier, reflects upon his mortality and the existence of God with his girlfriend, Sonja:

> BORIS: Sonja, are you scared of dying?
>
> SONJA: Scared is the wrong word. I'm frightened of it.
>
> BORIS: That's an interesting distinction. Oh, if only God would give me some sign. If he would just speak to me once. Anything. One sentence. Two words. If he would just cough.
>
> SONJA: Of course there's a God! We're made in his image!
>
> BORIS: You think I was made in God's image? Take a look at me. You think he wears glasses?
>
> SONJA: Not with those frames.[6]

I cannot overstate the importance of developing a pastoral reputation that refuses to shy away from honesty concerning difficult topics, especially as a preacher seeks to broach seminal (but relatively outrageous) ideas like reminding a congregation that they've already died in baptism.

Building trust used to shape such a radical sacramental identity requires unhurried and holy time and occurs gradually, as a pastoral leader probes difficult texts with theological honesty and candor over the course of several lectionary cycles. Although "believe me"[7] became the repeated mantra of a certain presidential candidate in the 2016 election, offering a preacher unquestioned authority will typically not transpire in parish life simply because the pastor is wearing a clerical collar.

"By what authority are you doing these things?" Jesus was once asked. "Who gave you this authority to do them?" (Mark 11:28). Not a bad pair of questions, regardless of their antagonistic source. It's interesting here that Jesus refuses to establish credibility by trotting out the equivalent of a seminary diploma or an ordination certificate to prove once and for all why he's to be trusted. His preaching style is not overly "authoritative" and conversation-ending but instead often open-ended, even intentionally ambiguous. Why?

I'm convinced Jesus laid aside his divine accreditation for the sake of others, inviting followers down a path of discovery that occurs with a very intentional teaching style. He will not spoon-feed his disciples. Nor will he attempt to make the complex instantly clear and forever settled.

Jesus "was in the form of God, but did not regard equality with God as something to be exploited" (Phil 2:6). Perhaps the man often refused to trot out his own sanctioned divine credentials because he knew it would get in the way of *other people* going to God. He brilliantly leaves us hints along the way, bits of bread along the path. But he wasn't looking for passive listeners of those teachings who would inherently swoon over his "authorized" version of wisdom. Jesus sought to release people from theological tethers controlled by appointed arbiters of final truth who "lock people out of the kingdom of heaven. For you do not go in yourselves, and when others are going in, you stop them" (Matt 23:13). I'm reminded here of a memory from the writer John Leax, recalling life growing up on his grandfather's farm:

> My grandfather Mimnaugh kept turtles for pets. He drilled holes in their shells near their tails and tethered them to trees with wires. In the evenings, while the adults talked, I watched the turtles at the end of their wires, straining toward the wild.[8]

Preachers, take note. One of the sermon's primary goals is not to elicit uniform agreement with a pastor's weekly ponderings. Like Jesus, we drop bits of bread along the path and release listeners to investigate together the wild truth of the kingdom of heaven.

Convey How the Preacher Has Already Died

"So we do not lose heart," Paul wrote to the church in Corinth. "Even though our outer nature is wasting away, our inner nature is being renewed day by day" (2 Cor 4:16). Over unhurried time, as a preacher establishes the congregational trust required to lead an assembly toward the audacious confession that I'm describing in these pages, it will be appropriate to offer from the pulpit instances of how such a sacramental death makes a difference in the daily discipleship of the bearer of such proclamation.

I'm not suggesting here a regular diet of heroic stories with the pastor at the center. But neither should a pastor remain silent in describing how his or her dying and rising in baptism greatly matters in the development and renewal of one's "inner nature." Personal illustrations can come off badly from the pulpit and sometimes seem like an exercise in "look at me" self-righteousness. A greater danger is the complete absence of testimony from a congregation's preacher. It should be apparent, from our pastoral words and lives, that dying in baptism with the Lord has resulted in a life filled with decisions grounded in holy risk and how the promises of Christ overcome the fears that attempt to arrest inclinations to act in his name.

Even while we were dating, my wife, Cindy, and I (now married for forty years) talked regularly about our desire to adopt children. Our first child, Hannah, was born to us after Cindy's pregnancy and delivery in the Shenandoah Valley of Virginia. I recall late one evening, when Hannah was almost two and in bed, how Cindy and I looked across the kitchen table at one another in our parsonage and talked about how we might continue to build our little family: "Are we really going to do what we've always talked about doing?"

There were a dozen reasons not to—limited resources; barely enough money to scrounge together a single plane ticket to an orphanage where we'd learned, through Lutheran Ministries of Georgia, about a five-month-old baby girl needing a home; the unknown challenges of raising an interracial family; the fear of flying into El Salvador, mired in a long war; and the quiet reservations of my ninety-year-old grandmother from South Georgia who (I later learned) asked my mother, "Well, just how dark is she?"

We prayed together—a lot. The decision to bring our second child, Marta, into our Virginia home ultimately hinged upon what we'd been taught about baptism. "We've been born in Christ for this," I recall Cindy saying. A kind man, Bob, in our congregation helped with the plane ticket. After a whirlwind trip to Central America for a young mom who'd hardly been out of the southern United States, Cindy and Marta stepped off the plane at Dulles airport in DC near Christmas in 1988 and were surrounded by a small community of friends and family. Hannah, the big sister, age three by then, said, "Give her some milk."

"Hear therefore, O Israel, and observe [his commandments] diligently, so that it may go well with you, and so that you may multiply greatly in a land flowing with milk and honey, as the Lord, the God of your ancestors, has promised you" (Deut 6:3). This verse precedes the powerful imperative instructions of the liturgical Great Shema about loving God with heart, soul, and might: "Keep these words. . . . Recite them to your children. . . . Bind them as a sign on your hand. . . . Write them on the doorposts of your house and on your gates" (Deut 6:6–9). It is precisely this land flowing with milk and honey—abundance even amid scarcity—that emboldens and fuels the Christian life.

"Give her some milk," said Hannah. Indeed, Marta brought her own milk of gladness into our lives. As would the girls' brother, Lukas, three years later, who arrived in our family via adoption when he was four days old, a biracial baby boy who also needed a home.

Our three children are grown now and working in respective vocations—public defense attorney, preschool teacher, and organic produce deliveryperson—in two Southern towns. Like any family, ours has had its set of challenges and hardships. We five, however, have been shaped throughout by the gift of baptism, a new family born out of a very old set of promises, one of which invites the baptized to take risks because of the One who's gone before us, even through and beyond death, and leads the way.

Stories like these should, of course, take a back seat to the centrality of the assigned and preached word. But similar shared testimony (from a pastor and others in the congregation) will undergird and strengthen pastoral proclamation in that parishioners will catch the holy joy and righteous nerve involved in following Jesus postbaptism. "Faith is caught, not taught," said a theologian whose name escapes me. Several families in one of our parishes, for instance, decided to build their households through adoption after hearing the narrative of our personal experience. Risks taken among those who've died in baptism become contagious.

Offer Sermons That Address Fear and Promote Shared Suffering

While cleaning the house one recent pandemic "shelter in place" morning, I felt the need to queue up some a cappella medieval chant and polyphony from the CD bin and settled upon *1000: A Mass for the End of Time* by the incomparably gifted quartet of women known as Anonymous 4. Haunting harmonies filled the house. The musical disc seemed to fit the national mood. A friend phoned in the middle of my dusting and asked about the music in the background. I explained about the pervasive fear that marked the late tenth century at the turn of the millennium and suggested it was somewhat similar to the worry currently outside our back doors. "You're an odd man," he said. During our conversation, I noticed the CD cover art for the first time—a large fish (recalling the Jonah story) swallowing several poor souls bound in chains.

Sermons will regularly address the various fears of listeners, partly because the lectionary returns like a drumbeat to the fears of disciples and the fears that fueled Paul's letters of comfort and catechesis, not to mention the fear associated with the Bible's final apocalyptic book, all informed and overcome by the love and promises of Christ:

> After this I looked, and there was a great multitude that no one could count, from every nation, from all tribes and peoples and languages, standing before the throne and before the Lamb, robed in white, with palm branches in their hands. They cried out with a loud voice, saying,
>
> > "Salvation belongs to our God who is seated on the throne, and to the Lamb!"
>
> And all the angels stood around the throne and around the elders and the four living creatures, and they fell on their faces before the throne and worshiped God, singing,
>
> > *"Amen! Blessing and glory and wisdom*
> > *and thanksgiving and honor*
> > *and power and might*
> > *be to our God forever and ever! Amen."*
>
> Then one of the elders addressed me, saying, "Who are these, robed in white, and where have they come from?" I said to him, "Sir, you are the one that knows." Then he said to me, "These are they who have come out of the great ordeal; they have washed their robes and made them white in the blood of the Lamb.

> *For this reason they are before the throne of God,*
> *and worship him day and night within his temple,*
> *and the one who is seated on the throne will shelter them.*
> *They will hunger no more, and thirst no more;*
> *the sun will not strike them,*
> *nor any scorching heat;*
> *for the Lamb at the center of the throne will be their shepherd,*
> *and he will guide them to springs of the water of life,*
> *and God will wipe away every tear from their eyes." (Rev 7:9–17)*

It was about 11:00 p.m. one Saturday night. I was walking down a trail through some woods in Maryland at Wellspring Retreat Center—connected to the Church of the Saviour in Washington, DC, led by the gifted pastor and writer Gordon Cosby (1918–2013)—conversing in the dark with two women from central Ohio about the Christian life and the hurdles adults often encounter in our parishes that block a deepening of discipleship. It was a great conversation; we walked along in the dark woods, enjoying a nice starry evening, chatting about church. The three of us eventually came upon our cabins, said goodnight, and went to our respective rooms. I locked the door out of habit and turned on a single light.

As I stood there beside my bunk, pulling on pajamas in the dim light, a hand suddenly shot out from under the bed and grabbed my bare right ankle. I yelled, or cursed, maybe both. Mark, a pastor friend, had been hiding under the bedsprings in an uncomfortable position, laughing softly, maniacally, for at least twenty minutes. (This act may give lay readers a clue concerning the warped depths of clergy psychosis.) We eventually laughed hard enough to draw the attention of the women from Ohio, but for just a split second, it felt like I was entering a Stephen King novel and that hand was dragging my life down into the Valley of the Shadow where no Good Shepherd could be of assistance.

People get pulled under the springs, so to speak, all the time. Some unforeseen hand of fate reaches out and life can change overnight. Cancer happens without warning. Committed and talented employees are fired unexpectedly. Long marriages break up, to the surprise of friends and family. Babies are born with severe challenges. Pastors and their parishioners face myriad agonies together that can quickly upset a full, vibrant faith and leave people wondering if there is a benevolent God behind the endless suffering in the world.

"Yes, this is a hard life," one pulpit response goes. "A lot of stuff happens we can't explain. But one fine morning in the future there will be no more hunger or any scorching heat and God will remove all your sad tears. We'll worship God day and night within his temple. Won't that be something, a great and fine Hallelujah filled with endless joy?" I've always appreciated Mark Twain's wry response to such a saccharine promise:

> In man's heaven, *everybody sings!* . . . And *everybody stays*; whereas in the earth the place would be empty in two hours. . . . In the earth these people cannot stand much church—an hour and a quarter is the limit, and they draw the line at once a week. . . . And so—consider what their heaven provides for them: "church" that lasts forever and a Sabbath that has no end![9]

Twain died a bitter man—partly due to a daughter who drowned in the bathtub one Christmas Eve during a seizure. *Letters from the Earth* (the source of the previous quote) was not released for publication by Twain's family until well after his death, but the man never tried to hide how pious promises of a pain-free heaven to soften the blow of suffering in this life just didn't do a whole lot for him.

The careful preacher will approach biblical descriptions of heaven with utmost care, especially when employing such imagery to address fears that may be lurking under the bedsprings and tucked away in closets. The long passage I've cited from Revelation resembles a scene from some epic movie set. "*Who are these?*" asks an elder. These palm branch–wavers who've come through "the great ordeal" (Rev 7:14) are early Christian martyrs, singing, fresh from recent suffering.

Heaven is not blissfully removed from the world's pain in a fashion that erases the suffering we've been through in the past. Recall again the powerful scene in John's Gospel where the resurrected Jesus appears to the skeptic Thomas and his pals on that first Easter. Jesus shares needed peace with his friends (Thomas is absent for this first visitation) and then immediately "show[s] them his hands and his side" (John 20:19–20). A part of me wishes all that terror and pain was now forever air-brushed from the man's identity, but Jesus refuses to separate perceived peace from his past suffering. A week later (20:26)— the time-lapse surely says something about the early church's patient tolerance for doubt voiced in community—Jesus again appears to the disciples, and Thomas is present for a repeat offering of the Lord's healing peace coupled with a bold parading of his wounds (20:26–27). For many years, I thought this text was centrally about healthy doubt in the life of a disciple. The story certainly addresses this topic but perhaps principally offers clues concerning how honest conversation about and sharing of communal wounds affords skeptics authentic glimpses of the resurrected body of Christ, the church. There is something powerful about this connection between the peace offered by Jesus and the wounds he makes no attempt to hide. Authentic peace, Jesus seems to be illustrating, cannot occur in congregational life until church members dare to reveal and share one another's pasts and common scars.

"Baptism," writes Rachel Held Evans (1981–2019), "declares that God is in the business of bringing dead things back to life, so if you want in on God's business, you better prepare to follow God to all the rock-bottom, scorched-earth, dead-on-arrival corners of this world—including those in your own heart—because that's where God works, that's where God gardens."[10] Baptism, suffering, and God's peace are intimately intertwined.

These are not Pollyanna palm wavers. Note also this paradoxical heavenly detail from the Revelation text: "For the Lamb at the center of the throne will be their shepherd" (7:17). "The Lord is my shepherd" but also, apparently, a crucified lamb. At the very center of heaven is the shocking surprise that the singers have not only suffered and are still shaped by such suffering, but they are also *singing to a sufferer*, their shepherd, the Lamb, who chooses their lot and "will guide them to springs of the water of life," a phrase resounding with sacramental implications. No need to fear who's hiding under the bedsprings when the Lamb's followers are relentlessly led to baptismal springs by a man who faced death and came back from it. Tom Long writes,

> The Christian faith intends to blur the boundary between the dying and the living. . . . In baptism, new Christians die with Christ, which is a sign of hope. We have already died, we have already experienced the worst that can happen to a human being, and by dying with Christ, we also participate in the promise that we will rise with Christ. But to place a symbol of death at the very beginning of the Christian journey is also a sign of realism. It reminds us that we are not permanent and immortal, that we are made of dust and to dust shall we return.[11]

The saints in light sing with the crucified Lamb, celestial choral joy not entirely removed from their suffering but instead shaped by its steely strength, a strange power made perfect in weakness (2 Cor 12:9). "May you be made strong with all the strength that comes from his glorious power," Saint Paul writes, "and may you be prepared to endure everything with patience, while joyfully giving thanks to the Father, who has enabled you to share in the inheritance of the saints in the light" (Col 1:11–12).

Preach from a Providential Perspective

I have a close friend, Andy, who was returning home one fall after a long hike on the Appalachian Trail. Dog-tired and seeking sleep, he stowed his pack in the luggage compartment under a crowded Greyhound bus, climbed the steps to the first row of passengers, walked to the very back, and collapsed into a lone remaining seat. Every time Andy dozed off, however, a guy sitting next to the window woke him up and wanted to chat. "And here's a picture of my girlfriend waiting on me. Get a load of this," said the man, who'd just been released from prison. The picture revealed a lot more than Andy cared to view.

Several more attempts at sleep failed, particularly when the man removed his glass eye and waved it under Andy's nose. Later, the animated man even reached over the seat in front of them where two young women were sitting, the glass eye perched between his thumb and index finger. "I can see you! I can see you!" chirped the man to the two women. The driver stopped the bus and walked slowly all the way to the back, glaring at Andy and his seatmate. He threatened to throw them both off the bus "if these shenanigans don't come to an end." My friend was so tired he made no attempt at a defense and was finally able to sleep.

God sees us. We pray to "one who judges all people impartially according to their deeds" (1 Pet 1:17), both the living and the dead, according to the second article of the Apostles' Creed—God, the benevolent and all-knowing eye. "I can see you," the Lord says without jest, in love. It can be both terrifying and also a great relief to be seen so completely. In John's Gospel, the woman at the Samaritan well, suddenly an evangelist, seems pleased as punch to report to her neighbors that Jesus knows about everything she's "ever done" (John 4:29) and, presumably, will do. It can be liberating to be known and seen so completely and still loved and accepted.

Such a theological reality has great potential to shape the discipleship of a community of Christians who have already died in Christ in baptism and are now reborn to a loving God who knows us so intimately and well, not with the intent to punish, but rather to gracefully and powerfully guide. To be so utterly known surfaces another word that has gone out of vogue in many Christian communities: *providence*, literally a "seeing ahead."[12] This word, unfortunately, has been used in such a way to imply that all our paths and decisions have been mapped and decided for us without regard to human choice or volition—essentially, that we are Stepford disciples with no real choice in the matter. God can know our paths, however, without disciples signing up for robot-hood.

I've always loved the strange sequence of sailings, dreams, and revelations early in Acts 16 that lead Paul, Timothy, and Silas to Philippi and their first encounter with Lydia (16:14).[13] On this missionary junket, the Holy Spirit, in turn, "forbids" (16:6) the trio to speak the word in Asia, diverts an attempt to enter Bithynia (16:7), and ultimately convinces them via dream to set sail and assist a pleading Macedonian (16:9–10). I often long for such divine clarity in my own life, especially on the cusp of committing colossal errors in judgment. Aren't these examples from Acts, however, despite their compelling providential nature, instances of a controlling God who moves his servants around like willing pieces on a chess board?

I've recently learned the word *murmuration*, which describes a flock of starlings bending and turning in the late afternoon sky as a single unit in acrobatic displays that border on performance art featuring a large living Slinky. I love to watch starlings perform in early autumn, even though they're now an invasive species in America after someone (in 1890) released sixty of the birds in New York City's Central Park in an attempt to populate North America with every avian citation in the works of Shakespeare. Two hundred million starlings now grace the US skies. Fiction writer Karen Russell declares that a thousand of these birds can "bunch into a living fist over the trees, relax westward, shear away behind the eastern skyscrapers. With a kind of muscular clairvoyance, each bird seems to anticipate the movements of others. What is deciding them? What permits a thousand autonomous actors to move as one body, at these unbelievable speeds?"[14]

I've never pastored a church body that moved "as one" at unbelievable speeds, but *murmuration* is still an apt word to describe a congregation that listens intently for the direction of God's providential voice, "anticipating the movements of others."

God sees.[15] God acts. Christians are not deists, after all, who believe God wound up the world's machinations long ago like a clockmaker but now resides in heaven, watching it all unfold with distant consternation or unattached amusement. No, the Spirit hears our groans and "helps us" (Rom 8:26), interceding for the saints, the church, "with sighs too deep for words." We worship a God "who searches the heart" (Rom 8:27). These are not actions of a removed deity.

The church may stumble or rebel. "The old Adam is drowned in baptism, but that jackass is a good swimmer," said Luther, explaining the need to return daily to this postmortem baptismal gift. Postbaptism, dying and rising in Christ, the air the church now breathes is forever Spirit-inspired by a God who clearly sees the way ahead.

Employ Artful, Risky, and Parabolic Language

For over thirty springs—normally in late May on the Blue Ridge Parkway in North Carolina and Virginia—I've embarked on bicycle trips with an illustrious group of church guys known as "The Pannier People." We load our bike racks and saddlebags with camping gear and provisions (including a dram or two of whisky), say goodbye to our understanding wives, and pedal for six days through the beauty of the southern Appalachian highlands. For many years, we rode from Abingdon (where I served for a decade and a half) up the parkway to Roanoke College, the annual site of the Virginia Synod Assembly. Our bishop at the time, Richard Bansemer, once presented the cycling entourage with special padded seat pillows for the hard folding chairs dotting the assembly floor. Other years have taken us south on the parkway to Asheville (and beyond) via Mount Mitchell (elevation 6,684 feet), the highest point in eastern North America. Climbs on a loaded bicycle over thousands of feet in elevation change on the parkway can be brutal. Screaming descents rival the ecstasy of a roller coaster ride's release from a high apex.

One spring, planning a northbound trip back to Abingdon from a point originating several miles south of Mount Pisgah (named for the peak from whence Moses peeked into the promised land in Deut 34:1), we consulted the parkway website and noticed a landslide had closed a section of the roadway, suggesting a detour off the mountain down into Brevard—not much of a problem for a car but rather demoralizing for cyclists. "Surely the landslide can't be so bad," I said breezily. "We can always walk our bikes around it."

We reached the gated barrier on the parkway during the morning of day two. And a sign that read, "No Cars. No Bicycles." Undeterred, we pressed on. For several miles, the parkway was blissfully free of traffic—both lanes wide open, cycling heaven.

The landslide soon came into view. We dismounted and began pushing our bikes up and over large mounds of earth. A foreman high on the ridge stopped the large machine he was operating and called down, helpfully we thought, "Watch the tunnels!"

We waved up to him in appreciation. We'd always been careful in parkway tunnels—handlebar lights, flashing rear lights, all that. What we weren't counting on were the massive oversize trucks carrying earth off the mountain and then returning in rumbling ascent to load more—trucks that would not be looking for bicyclists in a dark tunnel on a closed road.

The first truck driver really let us have it. A creative verbal fusillade best not printed here. We picked our way down the mountain and regrouped, rather rattled, upon reaching the next "open" section of the parkway at the French Broad River, thankful our entourage made it safely through the landslide area.

Months later, in a group email, I conducted an online poll (an experiment, really) among our riders that consisted of a single question: "How many parkway tunnels did we travel through, with fear of meeting a large truck, between the landslide and the river? Don't look back at a map, answer off the top of your head."

"Five," offered two respondents.

"Four," answered another.

"Nine," said one cyclist.

The truth: we'd bicycled through just two dark tunnels, perhaps stupidly. Debatable, of course.

But please note for the record, dear preachers of God's word, what is not really up for discussion here: *fear warps and attempts to reshape reality.* Almost all the time.

What sort of language should the preacher employ to overcome fear and encourage daring risk grounded in the sacramental truth that we've already died in baptism? How with our words should pastors honor a God who once promised an apprehensive Moses, "I will be with your mouth and teach you what you are to speak" (Exod 4:12)? (My wife, Cindy, will attest that I'm a preacher who needs lots of help with his sassy mouth, in or out of the pulpit.)

In his whimsical and powerful pandemic prayer, James Parker asks the Lord to "let not heebie-jeebies become our religion, our new ideology, with its own jargon. Fortify us, Lord. Show us how. What would your saints be doing now?"[16] Theologian Lee C. Camp is surely correct about the preaching style of one saintly sermonizer:

> When Jesus went out preaching, he did not say, "Behold, I come declaring the true religion; embrace your personal relationship with me, and you shall enter heaven when you die." When Jesus went out preaching, he did not say, "Behold, I come declaring to you the means for you to know personal fulfillment and calm your existential angst." No, when Jesus went out preaching, he said, as the Synoptic Gospels summarize it: "Change! For God's kingdom is here."[17]

Jesus indeed preaches the need for changed and transformed lives, boldly and fearlessly grounded in a kingdom of grace, forgiveness, and reconciliation. Additionally, however, in his preaching and teaching, he models *how* God's word—"living and active, sharper than any two-edged sword . . . able to judge the thoughts and intentions of the heart" (Heb 4:12)—brings about such change.

Few listeners to sermons change direction through brow-beating and scolding. I cannot tell you how many people I've met—at parties, on elevators, and during bicycle trips—who've discovered that I'm a pastor and then quickly offered a defense of their departure from church as a result of captive weekly invective hurled from the pulpit by their childhood minister. Jesus does lose it at times, notably with the religious leaders of his day who attempt to make their converts "twice as much a child of hell" (Matt 23:15) as themselves. Revisit the entirety of Matthew 23 for a fiery eyebrow-singeing diatribe like no other in the Gospels that concludes with a sad lament over the holy city that Jesus loves. For the lion's share of his preaching, however, Jesus employs a different tack to access the depths of the heart where change can truly occur.

The parabolic preaching style favored by Jesus serves to draw listeners into a participatory exercise that engages heart and mind long after the story concludes. In fact, there often is no clear conclusion at all. It's rare that Jesus sits the disciples down to "explain" the one true meaning of what he just talked about. The stories Jesus tells are consistently elliptical in nature, colored by a provocative "dot-dot-dot" feel that plants pleasantly nagging detail in the lives of listeners (long after hearing the sermon) that works much like a seed or bit of yeast requiring time and germination to fully detonate, if ever. The parables seem to offer inexhaustible interpretive riches, an intentional polyvalence that appeals to a variety of listeners and perspectives.

One never discovers if the two brothers in the famous story of their generous dad ever reconcile (Luke 15:11–32). It's not clear if the sweaty and disgruntled grape pickers ever get over their self-righteous ire upon receiving the same wage as those who worked only a fraction of the day (Matt 20:1–16). No one steps forward in the parable of the weeds and wheat (Matt 13:24–30) to explain just how far a community should go in accepting "weedy" behavior in their midst. The tension between cheap grace, a rejection of legalism, and the value of spiritual discipline is never resolved in a parable about justification before God (Luke 18:9–14). A story that seems focused on holy behavior and the type of soil that best accommodates the word (Matt 13:1–9)—fairly clear-cut on the surface—can flip perspective in a wink and reveal an almost drunken seed-slinger who seems to take chances on landing places that any sane Burpee catalog gardener would discount with a glance.

The parables are intentionally open-ended and prone to head-scratching. This is part of their wisdom. Jesus's sermons were not windy and protracted, but an argument could be made that they lasted far longer than a stopwatch might be able to measure.

Jesus's disciples pose an understandable question to the parabolic preacher: *Why are your sermons shaped in this unusual fashion?* (Matt 13:10). His answer seems rather odd for pastors who desire to be understood with Sunday morning clarity and theological precision. "The reason I speak to them in parables is that 'seeing they do not perceive, and hearing they do not listen, nor do they understand'" (Matt 13:13), a paraphrase of God's address to Isaiah (6:9–10) after he experiences liturgical fireworks in the temple one Sabbath morning featuring melodic seraphs, hot coals purifying his reluctant lips, and a reminder that the holiness and glory of the Lord fill not only a defined worship space but also the whole earth. Jesus's answer to his disciples, then, suggests that a preaching ministry among the perception-and-hearing-challenged (any era, but perhaps especially screen-stricken residents of the twenty-first century) will require patience, nuance, time, and space not limited to the worship hour. If only "the hem" of the divine robe completely "filled" that temple (Isa 6:1), there's a lot of God waiting to be experienced outside its confines. It makes perfect sense, therefore, to avoid sermons that are tightly wrapped up with a telegraphed meaning and conclusion.

A proclamation that sends listeners to the door and down the steps and into the streets with a nagging realization that "this sermon isn't through with me yet" has a much better chance to mimic the sacramental action of dying and rising already effected in baptism. Like the water that finds its source in the temple and only gets deeper and more nourishing upon departing the building (Ezek 47:1–12), baptismal preaching, decidedly parabolic in the sense of open-ended polyvalence, will linger with the listener long into the week. "Everything will live where the river goes" (Ezek 47:9), a promise foreshadowing life for the baptized who have already died in Christ.

Learn from Poets and Fiction Writers

Consider this passage from *The Bones of Plenty* (1962), a novel about the challenges of North Dakota farm life during the Great Depression:

> Rachel seized a tail by either hand, walked out on the porch, swung her hands as far behind her as they would go, swung forward again with all the momentum the backward swing had given her, and let go of the cats. They lit running at least fifteen feet away and never stopped until they disappeared into the barn. She stood on the porch, watching them go, feeling still in her fists the narrowing vertebrae of their tails under the soft long hair and the thin warm skin, seeing still the way the tails had pointed in the air over the kitchen table as the cats ruined her pies.[18]

Even if you're unable to read another sentence from her excellent book, novelist Lois Phillips Hudson (1927–2010) paints here a vivid picture of a depressed rural economy on the brink of collapse. Rachel, a young mother and wife, has left the screen door ajar, allowing forbidden entrance for two cats that usually sleep under the front porch. Using an economy of words, the writer conveys several powerful realities in only three sentences—the frustration of personal negligence and subsequent anger over lost resources and wasted time; Rachel's own sense of airborne economic helplessness, completely out of her control and embodied in the flying cats and clenched fists; and the foreshadowing of even leaner times suggested by the boniness and "thin warm skin" of the two hungry creatures. The reader can clearly see Rachel's face, her angry windup, and the flight of the felines in slow-motion until gravity and fear send them scampering.

For good writers (and effective preachers) every word counts. "Precision," writes novelist Bret Lott, "is *the* most important element to crafting a piece of prose—and to crafting a poem, in fact, to crafting *any* piece of writing, from an obituary to a grocery list to the name you give a new file on your computer."[19]

Precision matters in preaching because worshippers do not settle into seats in the nave as completely settled people. We all (including the preacher) bring various worries and distractions with us on Sunday mornings. Worries that bang their various drums in our imaginations, competing for attention with interior volume—next week's presentation, tomorrow's test, yesterday's argument, a doctor's diagnosis. Preachers are still graciously offered the attention of most listeners as the sermon begins. It's easy, however, to lose listener attention and painfully obvious to detect from the pulpit when the drums seem to be winning the day.

Poets and fiction writers have much to teach preachers in pricking and holding listener attention, especially as the sermon seeks to broach the reality of sacramental dying and rising under discussion here. Four considerations:

1. *Pay attention to sermonic entry points.* Take a quick peek at openings from short stories by authors who are masters of the form—Eudora Welty, Lorrie Moore, Ernest Gaines, Tobias Wolff, Flannery O'Connor, and Ron Rash, to mention a few. These and other short story writers offer just enough provocative detail to set a tone. "The child stood glum and limp in the middle of the dark living room while his father pulled him into a plaid coat,"[20] writes O'Connor

in the opening sentence of her story "The River," cited earlier in this book. O'Connor immediately gains access to the
reader's imagination. Where is the child going at this dark
hour? Why is he "glum and limp"?

A short story and a sermon differ in marked ways, but
their relative brevity suggests several intersections of com-
monality. A moving story and an effective sermon both
begin by dropping just enough bits of bread along a path of
discovery, pulling a reader/listener along. Both pique curios-
ity and leave one wondering about direction and resolution.
Both rely on the power of imagery and symbol. "Because
they were boys," writes Ron Rash in the opening sentence
of one of his stories, "no one believed them, including
the old men who gathered each morning at the Riverside
Gas and Grocery."[21] Rash offers just enough elements of a
scene, near water, inviting a reader to enter a tale that might
require suspension of what seems real, borrowing the eyes
of children to see something new.

2. *Avoid telegraphing the path of discovery.* Far too many sermons begin with too much information concerning content: "Today I'd like to talk about the dangers of adultery
by tackling the three main mistakes of King David after he
sees Bathsheba bathing on that roof in the book of Second Samuel." Right off the bat, a listener knows the sermon
topic and how many royal mistakes to listen for—a sure
invitation for a wandering mind to think about other things
while waiting for the preacher to discuss David's next wrong
turn. The best preachers (and best fiction writers) are those
who know where their theme is going but honor listeners
as companions of mutual discovery of truth that is revealed
slowly. The best movies, novels, and stories (and sermons)
share this in common: we're not exactly sure what happens
next, but we're given just enough "reveal" to keep listening.

3. *Give listeners something to think about or question during the sermon that does not have an easy answer.* My best teachers (similar to our best fiction writers) raised questions and ponderings in our time together that continued well after a class concluded, sending me to the library or into the deeper recesses of my brain for further examination and reflection. Sermons surface issues of human purpose, ethical responsibility, undeserved grace, the dilemmas of discipleship, and many other themes that are not easily resolved in fifteen minutes. My wife's childhood preacher employed a formulaic ending to every Sunday sermon she ever heard him preach: "Well, I've rattled on long enough today and I'd like to wrap it all up like this." Again, recall Edmund Steimle. Sermons wrapped up every week with a tidy bow rarely lead much to anywhere except reliance upon the preacher for a bit of weekly fast food.

4. *Do not assume biblical literacy.* A preacher soon discovers that even the details of the most famous Bible stories may not be well known. Furthermore, "We don't deeply inhabit the religious stories we do know. We aren't open to letting stories of faith and the movements of the spiritual life work on us."[22] Again, sermons can benefit from the meticulous attention to the power of narrative offered by short story writers.

Exploring the details of a story like Jacob's reunion with Esau after twenty years of estrangement (Gen 32) not only teaches the content of the tale but also offers an opportunity to examine motives of the principal character that are not explicitly detailed in the text. In this case, what does it say about Jacob that he crosses the river in the middle of the night with a large family entourage (32:22) and then hikes back across the river to sleep alone? Why does he send a massive zoo-like variety of animals ahead to his

approaching brother—550 beasts, by my count (32:13–15)?
Who exactly wrestles with Jacob in the night? A man, an
angel, God, or maybe even Esau himself? All four seem
possible in a titanic match that leaves our hero outmatched
(32:24–30) and walking with a limp.

I offer these four considerations shaped by the work of poets
and fiction writers because preaching that seeks to form a congregational identity of baptismal dying and rising is an enterprise that will face unconscious resistance and require unhurried
time for maturation. One of Emily Dickinson's poems begins
with the curious words, "Tell all the truth but tell it slant." *All
the truth*. That's quite an imperative invitation for any writer,
any preacher. Especially given the reality that few people will-
ingly embrace "in-your-face" truth consistently offered declara-
tively and prophetically. Lasting truth (in baptism, we have died)
requires artful revelation and unexpected surprise, often told
"slant" with homiletical creativity, patience, and prayer.

~~~~~~

Preaching is a scheduled liturgical extension of pastoral care
offered throughout any week. Pastors take not just themselves
but also the very word of God, portably, into living rooms, emergency rooms, hospice rooms, retreat settings, and a string of
seemingly endless meetings—the same living word that accompanies pastors into pulpits each Sunday morning. The authenticity of the ordained leader during the sermon shapes the trust
parishioners offer their pastor at other times of the week. And
vice versa; this parish trust accompanied by attentive listening
and postworship conversation shapes pastoral authenticity and
summons courage for daring and fresh proclamation. All settings potentially reveal opportunities for a pastor to teach sacramental identity, reminding people of who they are in baptism.

The Foothills Trail in South Carolina connects Oconee and Table Rock State Parks over a stretch of seventy-seven miles through surprisingly rugged mountains in the northwest corner of a state known for beaches. There is a section of the trail (about twenty-five minutes by car from my house in Walhalla) I would often hike when saddled with a problem in the parish that required even more prayer than usual. It wasn't that hard to slip away from town with an apple and a collection of poems (Wendell Berry and Luci Shaw were frequent companions) for a couple hours, sans cell phone. During the week, I hardly ever encountered people on this trail, which wound through hardwoods and along sweeping views toward the Carolina Piedmont before descending to a hidden campsite on a minipeninsula, surrounded by a curling and gurgling creek, where I'd sit and pray and think and read. I've often used this campsite on three-day backpacking trips with church youth groups as we raised money for the ELCA World Hunger Appeal.

The curious thing about this creek is its source just below the path about a quarter mile before the campsite. I've hiked this section dozens of times, but each time I take great delight in listening for the gurgle of water emerging suddenly from an invisible place in the hillside—a gentle babble sounding from silence, then gaining strength as the trail continues to descend. There is something about this sudden emergence of water from a hidden source that always shaped my prayers and gave perspective to the particular problem that caused me to board my Toyota Corolla and get out of town for a while.

Perspective is a hugely underrated gift. We (and our problems, conflicts, and worries) are around on this earth for the relative blink of an eye compared to the long unfolding of cosmic time. Paleontologist Stephen Jay Gould (1941–2002) once compared all earthly geologic time to the "King's Yard," the distance between the royal shoulder and the tip of his middle finger at the end of an outstretched arm. Take a nail file and make a single pass across that middle fingernail, Gould suggested imaginatively. The miniscule bits of nail that drop to the floor represent the amount of time, in relation to the King's Yard, that humans have lived on the planet.

This perspective in no way diminishes the anguish I (or a parishioner, or entire congregation) may be going through at the moment, but such perspective always serves to quiet and recenter me. "For God so loved the world" begins one of the most famous verses in the New Testament (John 3:16), an even more stunning move by this enamored God upon discovering that the Greek word for "world" is *kosmos*. There is no telling how long the water that gurgles mysteriously out of the bank below my favorite trail has been flowing and slowly carving the little peninsula upon which I sit to pray. We fill our church fonts with such grace and proclaim the radical promise that baptismal death in such flowing waters ushers those marked with the wide love of Christ's cross into a fantastically broad theological enterprise that far eclipses the years we've each been given here. Perspective is indeed a vastly underrated gift.

God's word is so saturated with stories of water and imagery of saving hydration that I halfway expect the worn and duct-taped binding of my Harper Collins NRSV Study Bible to splash my writing desk with visible drops whenever I gently pick it up for study or devotional use. Almost eight hundred references to water appear in the two testaments and the Apocrypha,[23] many more than popular words such as *hope* and *faith*. The potential for these water references to be used in preaching and pastoral care is vast.

Water appears first at the dawn of creation (Gen 1:2), well before the sky, dry land, and celestial lights. The great flood (Gen 7) "prefigures" baptism (1 Pet 3:20–22), drowning of sin, and rising in Christ. God reveals water and a well, obscured by Hagar's hopelessness and grief (Gen 21:19), now given fresh perspective with new sight. Moses is rescued from a floating "basket" (Exod 2:3)—a word used only here at the Nile River and earlier to describe the floating ark of Noah—foreshadowing future servants of God being plucked from the water for important callings. Water envelops the pursuing Egyptian army (Exod 14:26–28), and a new community of people emerges safely on the far shore, a text read at the Great Vigil of Easter to recall and enact the power of baptism. Naaman, the Aramean army commander, dips his proud heinie in the Jordan River seven times (2 Kgs 5:14), demonstrating the leveling and purifying effect of water. Postexile, at the Water Gate, Ezra gathers a despondent people who listen to the reading of Scripture (and preaching!) "from early morning until midday" (Neh 8:3) in one of my favorite texts from the Hebrew Bible that stirs the imagination of my liturgical-word-and-sacrament-heart (even though such a revival would perhaps clear the room of most Lutherans during the second hour). The Psalms are drenched with water, rivers, and springs. A prophet's wet vision where "everything will live where the river goes" (Ezek 47:9) describes a deepening stream whose source is located in a worship space. It's only in "deep water" (Luke 5:4) that hapless fishermen finally fill nets. The ancient well Jesus teaches beside in Samaria (John 4:1–41) overflows with themes of inclusion, forgiveness, and mission for a new disciple who winds up evangelizing her entire community. Even in the desert (Acts 8:36), water welcomes into a new household a marred man who has no family. The Bible's final chapter closes with a vision of "the river of the water of life" (Rev 22:1) flowing from the throne of God and the Lamb.

A dozen watery texts among hundreds.

I suspect a preacher could embrace the danger of taking too much license in making baptismal connections with biblical texts, as does Saint Ambrose in this rather unconvincing homily on 2 Kings 6:1–7: "When the head flew off the ax of Elisha's son as he chopped down a tree, it fell into the Jordan. But at Elisha's prayer it floated up. This is another type of baptism. Why? Because the unbaptized man is like iron weighed down and submerged. But when he has been baptized, he is iron no longer but is buoyant by nature like the wood of a fruit tree."[24] Even so, the Bible's saturation with images of water and new life provides a rich tapestry for sacramental preaching and opportunities to shape and strengthen a congregation's identity grounded in baptism.

The abundance of these liquid Bible stories reminds me of the refrain of one of my favorite John McCutcheon songs, "Water from Another Time":

> *It don't take much, but you gotta have some*
> *The old ways help the new ways come*
> *Just leave a little extra for the next in line*
> *They're gonna need a little water from another time*[25]

Plagued with images of mortal fear, images that accompany parishioners into worship each Sunday and into the week, any congregation greatly benefits from pastoral care that's baptismally immersed in the teachings and promises of Jesus who "might destroy the one who has the power of death, that is, the devil, and free those who all their lives were held in slavery by the fear of death" (Heb 2:14–15). People held in slavery "all their lives" in such a manner are liberated from fear by ongoing sacramental catechesis centered upon a baptismal death that has already occurred. Through baptism, we are grafted into the body of Christ, who is "with [us] always, to the end of the age" (Matt 28:20).

I'm aware of one congregation in a small midwestern town where most church members reside their whole lives. After any baptism, the entire congregation processes, singing, into the church cemetery with the newly-baptized person leading the way—carried, in the case of an infant. The procession stops at the family grave plot. Prayers are offered. All make the sign of the cross in remembrance of their own watery welcome. The abundant sacramental water used that morning during worship is poured directly onto the grave plot where the newly baptized person will one day rest, awaiting the full resurrection of all the saints—a rising that has already commenced via the liquid death that just occurred inside the church building.

Numerous opportunities exist for pastors to teach and preach such a sacramental reality. These opportunities find grounding in the practices and theology of baptism communally shared in church life. In the next chapter, I'll examine ancient baptismal practices from the early church and how such old habits can enliven and liberate congregations like ours.

4

Shaping Local
Baptismal Practice

～～～

> Baptism isn't a capsule that transports us to the
> end of the road. Conversion is not an arrival at
> our final destination; it's the acquisition of a
> compass.
>
> —James K. A. Smith

I recall a church council meeting one winter evening many years ago in one of my parishes. On the agenda that night was an item that took most of the meeting to discuss. The Singleton[1] family in our congregation was not at all happy with me.

A Singleton grandson, William, born in a city two hours away, had recently made his planetary debut. I'd learned third-hand that a baptism would be "performed" on a certain Saturday night in our church sanctuary with only family members present to witness the event. A retired Lutheran clergy-relative would preside. "This is the way the Singleton family has always done baptism," I was told.

I called the grandfather, Tom—an active member of our church and former council member—and shared some of my pastoral concerns. We set a time to meet in my office at the church. Tom's wife, Susan, long inactive in the congregation, would accompany him. As soon as they arrived that Tuesday morning, I could tell our chat together would not go well.

Our baptism policy (two years old, but definitely in place) was quite clear on several items. All baptisms, unless there was a medical emergency, occurred on Sunday mornings at one of our six scheduled baptism festivals connected to the theology and rhythm of the church year. These dates were well-publicized months ahead of time so that prebaptismal planning and instruction for parents, sponsors, and others could occur. "Your grandson is joining the church," I told Tom and Susan. "Baptism is not so much a Singleton family moment but rather William's welcome into the wider body of Christ." (I didn't mention that William would die and rise with Christ in baptism. So judge me.)

Arms were crossed that morning in even further objection, surpassing the intensity that began the meeting. Two sets of eyes were starting to burn holes through their pastor.

There would also need to be a clear understanding, I shared, that the child's parents are connected to a congregation in their own town where they can fulfill the promises they'd be making in the baptismal liturgy: "to live with William among God's faithful people, to bring him to the word of God and holy supper, and to place in his hands the holy scriptures," among several specific parental pledges. "We can celebrate the baptism here in town at our church," I told Susan and Tom, "but there will need to be a body of people, a congregation, back home where William can grow and thrive in Christ. I'll need to be in touch with that pastor."

There would be no congregation for William, they said. Not now, and not in the near future. "You can't take this away from us," Tom said angrily. "You disappoint me, Pastor. I thought we called you here to serve us. I don't think you're doing that."

Broaching a common misconception, I gently reminded Tom and Susan that a pastor is centrally called to serve Christ in the community with the congregation, not so much specific families.

They didn't like that either. At the end of our meeting, I tried to pray; they declined. Saint Paul's rather sobering pastoral question came to mind: "Have I now become your enemy by telling you the truth?" (Gal 4:16).

Tom and Susan left my office that day in a huff. Phones lit up across the congregation. The evening church council meeting was called. The Singletons, five of them (grandparents, parents, and William the baby, fresh from a nap during the two-hour journey from his upstate home), made their spirited case for the Saturday night private baptism with emotion and some volume. William was raised aloft for all to see—a cute kid. We listened patiently, asking questions, offering alternatives. After their testimony, the Singleton family departed into the night with additional glares aimed at their pastor. Our church council conversed some more and prayed together. We then took a vote and unanimously decided to uphold and abide by the congregational baptismal policy. Our council president phoned Tom that night and shared the decision and our rationale.

The Singletons left our church and never returned. William's baptism occurred at another nearby church building on a Saturday night a few weeks later. I eventually received a note in the mail from the retired pastor-relative who presided at the private baptism. He told me it was possible to "attract more flies with honey than vinegar." I smiled at the peculiar evangelism advice from an older colleague and recalled, rather wickedly, that *Beelzebub* literally means "Lord of the Flies."

The whole saga required immense pastoral energy. Looking back, a few questions surface: *Isn't just the simple desire to be baptized, under any circumstance, enough in the eyes of Christ? Why not baptize indiscriminately and with full abandon? Maybe with a fire hose splashed into a willing crowd of penitents on a street corner? Was all that energy, time, and hard feeling really worth it?*

I'm starting this new chapter a couple mornings after President Trump departed the White House, dispatched peaceful demonstrators with tear gas, crossed the street, and held up a large Bible in front of Saint John's Episcopal Church like some magic totem revealing his and the nation's faithfulness. He juggled God's word slightly, admiring its heft. With a solemn and grave narrowing of serious eyes, our president hoisted for the cameras a book that he rarely opens. I told a friend that if future historians go searching for an example of the regrettably retired word *blasphemy*, they need look no further than this staged scene. William Stringfellow, cited earlier, came to mind: "The weirdest corruption of contemporary American Protestantism is the virtual abandonment of the Word of God in the Bible."[2] In this case, the word *virtual* could be changed to "literal." I had to laugh one night this week when Jimmy Kimmel replayed a tape of the whole Saint John's scene and ended it with a lightning bolt from heaven that incinerated the perceived magical prop and its proud holder.

How will the church remain faithful to its radical and inherited baptismal identity in an era that's rather weak on commitment? Doesn't a church of grace run the risk of alienating people like the Singletons by requiring anything at all? Given a Christian witness in our culture that is often about as deep as a pizza pan, is it not fair to ask who is excluding whom here? How have we gotten to such a state? When, who, and how should a congregation baptize?

A couple weeks prior to the protests sparked by the death of George Floyd from police brutality in Minneapolis and the subsequent raising of the presidential Bible on Lafayette Square across from the White House, I'd coincidentally started reading two excellent books—one on the Memphis assassination of

Martin Luther King Jr. and the international manhunt for his killer in the spring of 1968[3] and another (a novel, often whimsical) depicting the life and times of John Brown,[4] the curious Christian abolitionist who led an armed insurrection on a Harper's Ferry armory in 1859 that catalyzed the coming dawn of the Civil War. Describing events over a century apart, the two books revealed our entrenched history of national racism and various attempts to resist and combat (and also defend and promote) such racism. Both books spoke to the current events spooling out powerfully on the evening news in June of 2020. Both books revealed two men, King and Brown, whose faith in God and love for the Bible moved them to action in very different ways—King preached nonviolence to the very end; Brown took up arms for a cause he felt was unwinnable without them. Both men sensed an acute and fearless calling from God and a premonition that their deaths were inevitable due to their beliefs.

Author Hampton Sides recounts the agony of King's parents, listening to the radio in Atlanta at Ebenezer Baptist Church the night their son was killed. This touching scene reminds me of the power and importance of the promises any parent makes for their child at baptism. One wonders if a man like King could have emerged on the American scene without his classic spiritual formation in a Christian congregation. God shapes and calls disciples from an early age:

> Daddy King removed his glasses, and the tears coursed down his cheeks, toward his gray-flecked moustache. . . . He could only think of his son as a child, growing up, like his mother before him, in this very church, his young life revolving around Ebenezer. "My first son, whose birth had brought me such joy that I jumped up in the hall outside the room where he was born and touched the ceiling—the child, the scholar, the boy singing and smiling—all of it was gone. And Ebenezer was so

quiet; all through the church, the tears flowed, but almost completely in silence."[5]

Near the end of James McBride's novel, John Brown, on the morning before his hanging, describes the ways of the Good Lord Bird (a woodpecker) to the young teenage protagonist, Little Onion, and why its feathers are special. The abolitionist's words, though fictional, remind me of the sacramental dying and rising inherent in baptism, rooted in the tree of the cross (1 Pet 2:24 RSV) that brings new life:

> "The Good Lord Bird don't run in a flock. He flies alone. You know why? He's searching. Looking for the right tree. And when he sees that tree, that dead tree that's taking all the nutrition and good things from the forest floor. He goes out and he gnaws at it, and he gnaws at it till that thing gets tired and falls down. And the dirt from it raises the other trees. It gives them good things to eat. It makes 'em strong. Gives 'em life. And the circle goes 'round."[6]

Like any follower of Jesus, John Brown and MLK were both flawed and fallible men whose attributes and shortcomings will long be debated and examined in the corpus of books describing the slow march toward racial justice in America. This much, however, is not up for debate: they were both passionate about their respective callings, grounded in baptism and committed to God's vision of equality, and did not fear the threat of coming death. "Resurrection hope," writes Esau McCaulley, "doesn't remove the Christian from the struggle for justice. It empties the state's greatest weapon—the fear of death—of its power."[7]

Using the questions that concluded my description of a family whose insistence upon a "private" baptism was enough to precipitate their departure from our particular church community, the balance of this chapter will describe how baptismal practice in a local congregation has the potential of shaping disciples who fearlessly give their lives for Christ and his new community.

How Will the Church Remain Faithful to Its Radical and Inherited Baptismal Identity?

At one time in the Christian tradition, preparation for baptism was rather arduous and demanding. There was something at stake: "Whoever loves father or mother more than me is not worthy of me; and whoever loves son or daughter more than me is not worthy of me; and whoever does not take up the cross and follow me is not worthy of me. Those who find their life will lose it, and those who lose their life for my sake will find it" (Matt 10:37–39). Jesus requires radical allegiance for any would-be disciple, an allegiance that potentially brings division and reordering of the nuclear family as we know it:

> Jesus is not against family relationships, but he wants to know *who is first*. Please be clear: Jesus wants to be first not so he can punch your ticket into heaven. *Jesus wants to be first so that he can help you.* Help you in family life. Help you in your friendships. Help you in your job. Help you in an illness. Help you with that ornery neighbor you want to smack. Help you with a young person who is having trouble. Jesus will try to help you whether you place him first or fiftieth. The grace of Jesus is not contingent upon how we rank him in our lives. But practically speaking, Jesus will have a hard time getting to us if we place him fiftieth. And he will soon be fiftieth if he is not first.[8]

Preparation for baptism was arduous in the early centuries of the church because such radical reorientation is not possible through osmosis or luck. I'm aware that baptisms occur in the

New Testament with little or seemingly no preparation. "About three thousand persons" (Acts 2:41) were baptized at Pentecost in a single day. The Ethiopian eunuch (Acts 8:36) is baptized on a desert road following what appears to be rather express catechesis from Philip inside a moving chariot classroom. Perhaps the urgency of building a nucleus of what would become a formidable movement explains the brevity of early prebaptismal instruction. Certainly by the time of the writing of John's Gospel (ca. 90 CE) and after experiencing persecution from within (synagogue expulsion) and without (empire intimidation), a need to form disciples through a prolonged period of reflection and "counting the cost" seems to have emerged. Much fresco art associated with baptism focuses upon the lengthy Johannine stories of Nicodemus (3:1–21), the woman at the well (4:1–42), the man born blind (9:1–41), and the raising of Lazarus (11:1–44). A three-year period of preparation for baptismal candidates, the historic catechumenate, was not uncommon. Heidi Neumark describes a stunning bronze baptismal font she discovered at St. Mary's Church in Lubeck, Germany, on a trip to discover her Jewish roots. The font dates to 1337:

> The basin itself is held up on the shoulders of three kneeling angels. I knelt down, too, in order to see the figures in relief that wrap around the font in two bands. . . . The bottom band of figures portrays Adam and Eve, the temptation of Jesus, and his baptism. Between Adam and Eve and the temptation stands a very substantial devil that looks as if he's consumed large quantities of wurst, potatoes and beer. . . . A second ring of figures places the crucifixion squarely above Adam and Eve, with the trees of paradise and Golgotha entwined. Above the temptation comes Jesus' descent into hell and his reaching to rescue those who have not resisted temptation. On the lower band, Jesus' rising from the tomb parallels his rising

from the Jordan. The ascension follows with wonderful detail. As he ascends, Jesus' feet dangle below his robes, and on the mountaintop he leaves bronze footprints.[9]

Neumark notices a series of women she cannot at first identify: "The seven wise and seven foolish maidens came into focus. They paired up perfectly with the apostles—two bands joined in dance ringing around the font." Like many fonts from the Middle Ages, here was a deep well that taught sacramental meaning and biblical connection without words. Even in a preliterate era, baptismal catechesis carried a certain depth and theological rigor, equipping disciples with a new narrative that overcame even death.

It is worth quoting Garry Wills in some detail as he describes Augustine's baptism (with his mentor, Bishop Ambrose, presiding) in a large octagonal pool twenty feet across, from corner to corner, before dawn on Easter in Milan, Italy, in the year 387:

Augustine and his fellows gathered at the entrance to the baptistry, where Ambrose performed a ceremony of opening (Effetha) by touching their ears and nostrils, so that they would have a heightened spiritual awareness of what they were about to see and do. Then, just inside the baptistry, they faced west and renounced the devil, before facing east and welcoming the coming of Christ into their hearts. After this, they stripped off their clothes in one of the building's recesses, before being anointed with oil all over their bodies. . . . Then they stepped down into the baptismal pool, escorted by the bishop and his deacon, who ducked each person's head under the water three times as they professed belief in each member of the Trinity. As they came out of the pool, they were wrapped in a white garment signifying their innocence. They were anointed again, though this time only on the head. After that, the bishop washed their feet—a last gesture of exorcism, since the serpent in Eden had bitten Adam in the foot—then they received a "seal of the Spirit" and went to the New Basilica. For the first time, they heard the Lord's Prayer and participated in the Eucharist. . . . Baptism was a new beginning in a setting of new beginnings—at dawn (the beginning of day), in spring (the beginning of the year), on Easter (the beginning of salvation). Ambrose even thought that Easter occurred on the exact anniversary of the first day of creation (the vernal equinox).[10]

I make three observations concerning Augustine's lavish baptism with "his fellows," which included his son, Adeodatus, and close friend Alypius.

First, the time prior to the actual baptism was marked by a lengthy period of reflection and instruction. Nothing was rushed. This period certainly comprised what we now call "Lent" in the weeks before baptism but more likely covered a period of up to three years—plenty of time to "count the cost" of what it meant to sign on as a disciple of Jesus: "If any *want* to become my followers, let them deny themselves and take up their cross and follow me" (Mark 8:34). In any authentic conversion to Christ, there can be no subtle coercion or hint of evangelical arm-twisting. Converts must *desire* such a life, not be shamed or bullied into it. At the same time, Christ is crystal-clear about the demands of discipleship as a baptismal candidate relinquishes all competing allegiances, naming Jesus as "Lord"—a word in need of dire recovery here early in the twenty-first century as many Christians seem to bow the knee to a host of false political promises. Teachers like Ambrose in the early church did not seem interested in simply adding names to a congregational roll. Nuanced teaching marked by spiritual depth and catechetical breadth required time and patience from a variety of teachers but also gave candidates plenty of built-in checkpoints in the process leading to baptism to think hard about the nature of the life they were entering. Emotional manipulation in the name of "church growth" during this period—"Sinner, let go of that pew and come to Jesus!"—was rare.

Second, the depth and shape of the font in Milan (like the font encountered by Heidi Neumark in Germany) spoke volumes without words. I've noticed many smaller baptismal fonts in Lutheran churches across the United States with eight sides, but I often wonder if the numerical teaching potential of such fonts is often missed. Easter as the "eighth day of creation" clearly connects the sacrament to Christ's resurrection and his boundless love for a fallen world. Candidates entered the font in Milan via one set of steps and exited more steps on the opposite side. The anointing, the new clothing, and the depth of the pool all suggested a passage of dying to an old life and entrance into a new realm. A death has occurred, a drowning of the old person.

Third, Augustine's baptism in Milan conveys a clear paschal connection, the saving death of Christ, with the sacramental proclamation of Romans 6 and various reminders in Colossians (2:12; 3:3; 3:9–10). Death in Christ has occurred in baptism with a lavish welcome into his resurrected body, the church. Robin Jensen, in her impressive study of baptismal imagery in the early church, also notes that many ancient fonts were cruciform-shaped, "a design clearly meant to reinforce the idea that baptism was a participation in Christ's passion."[11] She quotes part of a baptismal homily by Cyril of Jerusalem (313–86) as he reflects upon Ecclesiastes 3:2:

> In that same moment you were dying and being born, and that saving water was at once your grave and your mother. What Solomon said in another context is applicable to you: "A time for giving birth, a time for dying"; although for you it is a case of

a "time for dying and a time for being born." One time brought both, and your death coincided with your birth.[12]

These three baptismal components appear over and again in the early centuries of the church. They are a large part of our rich and treasured sacramental inheritance: We count the cost. We die; we are drowned. We are born into a new realm.

Does a Church of Grace Require Anything at All Prior to Baptism?

The early church's emphasis upon lengthy catechesis and a sustained period of personal reflection for converts that led to a new and radical identity, marked by baptismal death and life in Christ, raises an uncomfortable question for many Lutherans and other Protestants: How does a congregation create a baptismal climate reflective of the richness of the early church without seeming legalistic? I suspect many pastors, laudably, desire to avoid any semblance of exclusion with a sacrament that's so radically inclusive: "As many of you as were baptized into Christ have clothed yourselves with Christ. There is no longer Jew nor Greek, there is no longer slave or free, there is no longer male and female; for all of you are one in Christ Jesus" (Gal 3:27–28).

A case can be made, however, that it's actually *inhospitable* to rush baptism (for an adult or with parents seeking baptism for a small child) in the name of "oneness" or inclusion. In many ways, new and active affiliation with a Christian congregation is like learning a foreign language. Inherently, there will be a period of confusion and head-scratching as this new language is first encountered. Instant accessibility to the ancient mysteries of the liturgy is neither possible nor desirable. Even for a sacramental savant, the many layers of baptism require a while to take hold, especially the rather shocking claim that the baptized have died in the waters of grace. Surely baptism, the sacramental jewel of the church's history, deserves plenty of time and loving attention in order to convey its depth and power. Is scheduling a baptism with next to no formal instruction or time for reflection a gesture of radical welcome or a sign of theological laziness on the part of congregational leadership?

After a long series of parables describing the kingdom of heaven, Jesus pauses and asks his disciples, "Have you understood all this?" (Matt 13:51). I think it's fair to imagine a sly grin forming around his mouth. "Yes," the twelve reply with a single word, an answer that has always struck me as rather amusing. Of course, they didn't understand it all. They couldn't upon first listen; no one can immediately grasp such teaching in all its fullness. Jesus then describes the powerful role of the teacher: "Therefore every scribe who has been trained for the kingdom of heaven is like the master of a household who brings out of his treasure what is new and what is old" (Matt 13:52). A catechist must be nimble, wise, flexible, patient, filled with spiritual depth, and grounded in ancient tradition.

Resistance to such a teacher and any protracted process leading to baptism should not surprise pastors. We live in an era of perceived express insight that often dabbles in various spiritual practices arranged for the masses like a pick-and-choose salad bar of theological options where the consumer is king or queen. Theological expertise shaped by years of study is sometimes called into question in a fashion akin to science denial.

I recall an uncomfortable telephone conversation with a man who called the church office one afternoon to ask if I might preside at his upcoming wedding. We knew each other a bit from various social encounters in our little town. Jeff was a nice guy, recently divorced. The date had been decided upon and the wedding would occur in his backyard that spring, a couple months away. I told Jeff I'd be glad to help if he was OK with our church wedding policy that included several sessions to plan the service and discuss the nature of marriage and the sacrificial promises he and his fiancée would be making to one another. I also shared that it would be important for me, a Christian pastor, to talk with them about the gift of communal life in a congregation and how marriages best thrive within a body of people who help the couple fulfill such radical vows over the long haul. Jeff's reaction was immediate and loud: "This is exactly why I'll never be part of any Christian congregation! You people all seem so exclusive and rigid! I thought pastors like you were always supposed to help and serve folk like me!" (The Singleton family again comes to mind.) I suppose an outsider could make the point that having any expectation at all attached to requested services leaves a pastor and congregation open to the charge of seeming "exclusive." But I hung up with Jeff that day and wondered, At what point can the opposite question be posed? *Who is truly excluding whom here?*

Part of the challenge in establishing a congregational process leading to baptism resides in the age-old tension between justification and sanctification.[13] Even acknowledging the many steps required to become proficient at playing the piano or learning the game of golf, it's still difficult for many Christians to admit that theological maturity requires a series of steps, disciplines, and percolated time. Christians do not arrive at theological maturity through osmosis or luck. The word *require* often sends Lutherans into orbit with charges of legalism and accusations of heresy grounded in the abandonment of "justification by grace through faith." The esteemed Lutheran theologian Gerhard Forde (1927–2005) once wrote, "Sanctification, if it is to be spoken of as something other than justification, is perhaps best defined as the art of getting used to unconditional justification wrought by the grace of God for Jesus' sake."[14] I greatly admire the man but will gladly go on record in disagreement with this statement.

If pastors and teachers are called to lead people toward an ancient understanding of baptism that includes the radical testimony of Romans 6, the idea of grace as "anything goes" in the name of inclusion must be aggressively and biblically challenged. Too much is at stake. "You have died, and your life is hidden with Christ in God" (Col 3:3)—a theological truth not embraced overnight or all at once. "Grace," writes Dallas Willard, "is not opposed to effort, it is opposed to earning."[15]

When? How? Who? Three Baptism Questions for Every Congregation

When?

Not only does the practice of rushed baptism with minimal or no preparation (except in the case of medical emergency) suggest a lack of hospitality from the host congregation, but such a practice is also arguably *unbiblical* given the breadth of the Great Commission. There are three clear directives here from Jesus (Matt 28:19–20) prior to his ascension: make disciples of all nations, baptize in the Trinitarian name, and teach them "to obey everything that I have commanded you." Granted, the word *everything* seems rather daunting, impractical, and perhaps impossible prior to one's watery welcome into the body of Christ, the church. Becoming a disciple of Jesus is a process that's never finished for any of us. Saint Paul sometimes speaks of salvation as a process: "For the message about the cross is foolishness to those who are perishing, but to us who are *being saved* it is the power of God" (1 Cor 1:18; see also 2 Cor 2:15). "Beloved, we are God's children now; what we *will be* has not yet been revealed. What we do know is this: when he is revealed, we will be like him, for we will see him as he is" (1 John 3:2). Pastors, liturgists, catechists, committee members, council members—all of us are together on the way "to maturity, to the measure of the full stature of Christ" (Eph 4:13). This is obviously not an all-at-once enterprise.

The connection between baptism and faithful catechesis, however, is abundantly clear in even the most basic understanding of this gospel road map, the Great Commission. Oddly, the church in my pastoral era has sometimes missed this biblical connection and evangelical opportunity. Teaching and training in discipleship will certainly continue, postbaptism, at any age. But the church that skips sustained and meaty teaching leading up to the baptism of a child or adult ignores a powerful window for catechetical welcome and inclusion. Something more than tradition (or perceived liturgical voodoo with benefits) has brought any baptismal candidate to this particular moment in time. It's vital for a congregation to think hard about the formational needs of those who are drawn to the font.

Some advice for congregations that practice infant baptism: strongly consider a series of baptism festivals, amply publicized, at the onset of any church year. Such a calendar allows plenty of time for planning, group reflection for parents and sponsors, and pastoral catechesis unpacking the theology of the sacrament and the meaning of various aspects of the baptismal liturgy.[16] The ancient "renunciation of Satan" within the liturgy calls out for extended conversation and understanding all by itself. Ample discussion is needed to explore the series of promises that parents and sponsors will be making on the child's behalf. The various liturgical elements of light, oil, and water all require time for percolation and reflection. Announced baptismal dates also allow a pastor's preaching ministry to be shaped by the appointed lessons in festivals such as Baptism of our Lord, Transfiguration, Easter Vigil, the Day of Pentecost,

Holy Cross Day, and other baptism dates decided upon by a worship planning team.

Many resources exist for parents, sponsors, and Christian Education teams as they faithfully welcome children into a congregation through baptism. An intentional sacramental refocusing may be called for in many locales, but excellent resources are plentiful. I'd like to focus the balance of this "when?" question, therefore, upon the baptism of adults.

Two very different congregations I pastored over a twenty-year period (one in a downtown South Carolina city and another in a small Virginia town) used "the catechumenal process" to welcome adults seeking baptism and others who'd been away from church life for a lengthy period of time and desired a deeper and more intense examination of the Christian life than typically offered in a six-week Inquirers' Class, which is certainly important in church life but often designed for fairly active Christians joining the congregation by letter of transfer. Similar to the process used by Pastor Paul Hoffman in Seattle for many years, ours was "designed both for those who have never been baptized as well as those who have at one time or another practiced a life of faith but have walked off, stomped off, or been chased off."[17]

Comprising four stages from early fall through the Day of Pentecost and based on the twentieth-century recovery of the ancient catechumenate,[18] the process as we adapted it required weekly meetings, public rites, service in the community, and regular worship attendance over a period lasting roughly seven months. Almost thirty years ago, George Hunter claimed that about one-third of secular, unchurched people are "ignostics," people who have "no Christian memory" and "don't know what Christians are talking about."[19] I suspect that percentage has risen in the intervening years, more acutely surfacing the need for congregational conversations of faithful welcome and a clear plan for evangelical hospitality.

What do people need who have not grown up in a Christian congregation or who've been absent since childhood? Join that question to an assumption that such folk are very often brought to a consideration of church life through transition or even crisis. It becomes clear that they've arrived at our church doors for reasons other than to admire our beautiful sanctuaries. The catechumenal process, in part, helps such a seeker discover *why* God has brought them. Factor in the central thesis of this book—that baptized people have already died in Christ and need not fear the future—and it becomes imperative that many congregations may need to reexamine local baptismal practices, particularly for adults.

Stage One of the process ("Inquiry") included a signed covenant that promises confidentiality, weekly attendance, and prayer for one another, among several other expectations and disciplines. Lasting much of the fall, the core of this stage centered upon the questions brought by the participants. Any question was fair game. *Who created God? Why is there so much suffering in the world? Why does it seem like my prayers never get a direct answer? Is there a heaven and hell? Why should I become a Christian and not a Buddhist?* The questions were typed and distributed and (with occasional magazine articles and readings) served as our curriculum for this first stage of the process lasting roughly eight weeks. A controlling verse for this first stage was John 1:38, the first words out of Jesus's mouth in that Gospel: "What are you looking for?" With his first disciples, Jesus began with the searching desire of those he encountered rather than trying to cram truth down their throats with religious facts they weren't asking about.

Stage One concluded with an honest discussion concerning whether participants wanted to continue in the process. A public rite on a Sunday morning in early Advent revealed to the congregation those seeking baptism or reaffirmation at the Easter Vigil, requesting prayer for each. I recall a young man named

Brian who announced one evening toward the end of the eight weeks that he was leaning away from receiving baptism. He agreed to pray for discernment during the coming week (as did the rest of the group). Brian returned the following Wednesday night with the news that he did not desire to be baptized. We prayed together and made clear to Brian that he was still welcome in the church community. Jesus's words again came to mind: "If any *want* to become my followers . . ." (Mark 8:34). There can be no coercive arm-twisting on any authentic path toward baptism. Brian departed the group with our blessing. His humor and insight were missed, but his clear conviction and heartfelt decision were honored. The catechumenal process, among its other benefits, gives a person time to consider whether baptism is the right spiritual fit.

Stage Two ("Deeper Formation") roughly coincides with the period from early Advent through the end of the Epiphany season. The controlling questions for this stage are, *With Mary of old, what's being born through me? With the magi, what gifts do I bring?*

Weekly meetings during this time are structured around one of the appointed texts for the coming Sunday, employing the ancient reflective Bible study method known as *lectio divina*, again using participant observations and questions to probe a story with depth that in turn heightens anticipation for Sunday worship and shows how the same text would be proclaimed in the liturgy through the sermon.

Churches cannot control how people come to faith any more than we can control how they lose it. We can only invite people into a real encounter with God's word and the grace of the sacraments. God cannot override human will in the calculus of faith and belief. God cannot ravish our intellects, our human decision-making. God can only coax and invite. This is part of the gift of *lectio divina*. Something happened long ago to Cleopas and his unnamed companion to make them hike the seven miles back to Jerusalem in the dark (Luke 24:33) after deciding to abandon the early Christian community: "Were not our hearts burning within us while he was talking to us on the road, while he was opening the scriptures to us?" (Luke 24:32). The catechumenal process offers space and time for inquirers to bring their holy questions to God. The process also provides space and time for God to bring the holy word to faithful questioners.

Stage Two is also characterized by the writing and sharing of a spiritual autobiography (one per week) by each member of the group. Again, the need for confidentiality is stressed. "My brothers and sisters, whenever you face trials of any kind, consider it nothing but joy, because you know that the testing of your faith produces endurance" (Jas 1:2–3). Naming and making sense of past trials is an important part of anyone's movement toward theological maturity. But often much of what a person has experienced can be painful, agonizing in retrospect, something other than joyful despite James's claim, requiring courage to share openly.

A man named Emerson[20] in one of our groups grew up in a very strict religious tradition that required the daily discipline of naming aloud each and every sin committed in the past twenty-four hours. He left the church soon after entering college and admitted that distrust of any religious authority often interfered with his consideration of a return: "I was so angry that I'd been bamboozled, and I was determined to never, ever be fooled again when it comes to religious belief."

Another participant seeking baptism, Mary, shared that she grew up with no church tradition at all. She recalled her first cross-country meet in high school when the coach led the team in the Lord's Prayer before the race: "Thank goodness that people look down when they pray because I knew only a few of the words."

Henry walked into our church sanctuary one Sunday early in the Pentecost season and began the catechumenal process the following fall. "I grew up in the Southern Baptist tradition, or lack thereof," he wrote in his spiritual autobiography. "I couldn't rectify the dogmatic gaps in the Baptist faith with the tools of mind-body-spirit that I had been culturally endowed with. I rebelled, turned to drugs and esoteric mysticism. I reconsidered the church at this juncture the way a person in a small rowboat approaching Niagara Falls might consider an island protruding upward into his clandestine path."

Emerson, Mary, and Henry, with many others arriving at our church doors, illustrate the need for a longer and more protracted process leading to baptism or reaffirmation. Again, the central issue here is hospitality and welcome and honoring the often-circuitous path down which God has accompanied the seeker and skeptic in all of us. "At the heart of baptism," writes Lee Camp, "lies an astonishing claim, an astonishing reality: all the division, all the social groupings, all the forms of identity that serve to categorize, divide, estrange, and alienate one from the other—these are broken down."[21] One of the gifts of the catechumenal process is that of holy time offered in service to the radical understanding of New Testament baptism and the developing trust in such divine promises. This trust, given the past agonies through which many have come, often cannot occur quickly.

Another public rite before the congregation on a Sunday in early Lent marks the beginning of **Stage Three** ("Intensive Preparation"). Lasting through the events of Holy Week and the ancient Triduum, this stage particularly focuses on these questions: *What is dying in my life? What am I leaving behind?* Weekly Bible study continues during this period with reflection on the classic spiritual disciplines. The group experiments with the discipline of fasting and discusses its challenge and liberation. We talk about varieties of prayer and how one form does not necessarily fit all. The spiritual benefits and need for sacrificial almsgiving in a broken world are openly discussed among group members who've gotten to know one another well over the last months.

Holy Week is always a highlight of the catechumenal process with so many rich and powerful moments and symbols—footwashing (led by members of the group) and the stripping of the altar on Maundy Thursday; the darkness of Good Friday, proclaimed and recalled via the shared reading of John's passion narrative; fire, darkness, light, and the water of welcome at the Great Easter Vigil through baptism and asperges (where everyone gets wet); the joy and festivity of Easter Sunday morning. Group members receive adequate instruction in order to prepare for this trio of services, but much is left for the group to experience as liturgical surprise and delight. There's always a lot to talk about as Holy Week concludes and the fifty days of Easter begin.

Stage Four also goes by the ancient name of *mystagogy*—an extended period of reflection on the sacramental mysteries of baptism and communion that coincides with the season of Easter. This stage is marked by another question: *What is alive in me now that I've died and risen with Christ in baptism?* Attention to spiritual gift discernment is a central part of this stage, leading toward the day of Pentecost, where group members stand before the congregation and offer testimony concerning their spiritual gifts and God's specific call now present in their lives. "God has not created a single person whose essence and uniqueness are not eternally needed," writes Gordon Cosby. "The person who is having the time of her life doing what she is doing has a way of calling forth the deeps of another. Such a person is herself good news."[22] Many new ministries began as a result of sounding respective calls by members of catechumenal process groups on Pentecost. Other church members were often attracted to the new ministries they heard described.

I'm sure there are other ways to faithfully prepare and lead an adult to (and through) the waters of grace in baptism. The ancient catechumenate, however, is a process[23] that offers the valuable gifts of time and accompaniment—in short, a process with depth, which leads me to question number two in every congregation's baptismal deliberations.

How?

Tadeusz Ostrowski opened his front door in Abingdon, Virginia, one Monday morning in early spring and was greeted by a bucket of cold water thrown in his face by his loving wife, Maria. "Happy Wet Monday!" she called out with three of the few English words she knew at that point. The Ostrowskis, Polish refugees resettled by our congregation through Lutheran Immigration and Refugee Service, were still new in our community. I'd never heard of Wet Monday but immediately fell in love with it.

In Poland and other European countries, the Monday after Easter is an especially common time to recall one's baptism and get pretty wet in the process. It caught on in the Honeycutt family and with several other households in the Saint John congregation, especially those with children. Easter Monday became a day to get soaked.

Baptism is a death—a paschal dousing. How congregations choose to convey such a sacramental truth matters greatly as the church year unfolds. The congregation in Abingdon began in 1962, temporarily gathering in a local funeral home until the first church building was complete. Children sometimes played hide-and-seek among the coffins when their parents weren't looking. I've often thought that this origin story from the church's early days helped shape the bold decision to build a baptismal font decades later that clearly conveyed images of dying and rising in Christ. We also held an annual outdoor service in the mountains near town that sometimes included baptism by immersion in a creek that ran behind the picnic shelter. Church members were creatively faithful in celebrating baptismal anniversaries, their "death dates" marking entrance into the body of Christ in light. (My own anniversary, July 28, 1957, is an especially enticing invitation to get wet in the heat of late July. I've celebrated with watery encounters ranging from a clandestine skinny-dip on a secluded section of the Erie Canal on a cross-country bicycle trip to hunting golf balls in a cold mountain stream in North Carolina near the eighteenth green with a nylon mesh collection bag, inviting full submersion. I stopped collecting, for the record, at exactly twenty-eight golf balls that day, an apt number.)

The Saint John congregation's eventual decision to build a large font at the entryway to the new sanctuary did not occur all at once. But events like Wet Monday, worship in a context associated with death, the embracing of new life from a cold creek behind the picnic shelter, and creative baptism anniversary celebrations all served to shape the decision that the small wooden font used for decades was no longer adequate to convey baptism's freedom from fear inherent in a saving act that is centrally about dying with Christ: "Now the Lord is the Spirit, and where the Spirit of the Lord is, there is freedom. And all of us, with unveiled faces, seeing the glory of the Lord as though reflected in a mirror, are being transformed into the same image from one degree of glory to another; for this comes from the Lord, the Spirit" (2 Cor 3:17–18). Baptism into Christ frees and transforms God's people. Crossing through the spacious narthex to the threshold of the entrance to the nave, we wanted to convey a feeling of entrance to a new land, much like crossing the Red Sea once created a whole new people bound for a promised land.

A small upper pool with moving water invites the dipping of a hand and a moist signing of a cross on one's forehead. A portion of John 4:14—"All who drink of the water that I will give them will never be thirsty"—is etched into the large stone through which water from below pumps silently to form this upper pool. The front of the stone is sloped. Water flows across the granite surface to fill the lower, larger pool. The image recalls Moses striking the rock in the wilderness from which water springs forth for thirsty people (Exod 17; Num 20). The lower pool (which can accommodate the baptism of an adult or child) is cross shaped with a flat wooden housing that invites a person to sit and linger. A beautiful cruciform mosaic in colorful tile adorns the bottom of the deep pool. The pastor leads the weekly Sunday confession from the baptismal font. All make the sign of the cross at the absolution to remember and recollect a common identity. It would be difficult for a guest to encounter this font and these practices without noticing that something here is different, liberating, and altogether strange in an American culture often bound by fear of death. This font conveys clearly that baptismal death has occurred and life in Christ has commenced.

How congregations celebrate and enact the baptismal rite reveals what is at stake when one signs on as a follower, a disciple of Christ. Thomas Merton describes his baptism in November of 1938 as his "happy execution and rebirth."[24] "Whoever you are," Merton continues, "the land to which God has brought you is not like the land of Egypt from which you came out. You can no longer live here as you lived there. Your old life and your former ways are crucified now."[25]

Even if a redesign of the baptismal space is impractical due to physical or financial restraints, copious amounts of water should be used to convey the baptismal drama of crossing the sea to a new land, the journey of death and rebirth. Phinney Ridge Lutheran Church in Seattle offers baptism by submersion in a metal livestock trough brought in for the Easter Vigil.[26]

Noting Luther's observation in *The Large Catechism* that baptism "consists of being dipped into the water, which covers us completely, and being drawn out again," slaying the old Adam, Anita Stauffer writes,

> Certainly the omnipotent God can effect salvation when only a few drops of water are used. However, if the Church is to recover the full and profound significance of baptism, then baptism must be done in a way that is consistent with its meaning: submersion in water. . . . Perhaps a congregation can only comprehend baptism as death and resurrection if the font holds enough water that an adult *could* drown.[27]

WHO?

Given my emphasis in these pages upon the radical death and new life enacted through such liquid and lavish welcome into the church, I suppose one could make the argument that Anabaptists should not be the only Christians insisting upon "believer's baptism," waiting until someone is old enough to discern what's actually occurring as the various components of sacramental celebration unfold. Wouldn't it make sense to wait and couple baptism with an extended period of teaching and reflection similar to confirmation? I've always liked Frederick Buechner's response to this concern: "If you don't think there is as much of the less-than-human in an infant as there is in anybody else, you have lost touch with reality. When it comes to the forgiving and transforming love of God, one wonders if the six-week-old screecher knows all that much less than the Archbishop of Canterbury about what's going on."[28] Baptism is centrally about God's action more than our comprehension of what's occurring. I've also always loved a story Will Campbell's father told him about a preacher in Arkansas who was asked if he believed in infant baptism. "Believe in it?" replied the preacher. "Hell, I've actually seen it."[29] Again, sprinkling an infant with an ounce of water is no less valid a baptism than the complete submersion of an adult who's committed for months to the catechumenal process. God acts. Christ unites us to his saving death. The Spirit offers gifts for ministry.

Having said this, indiscriminate baptism (except in extreme or emergency circumstances) is not a great idea. If there are no sponsors or parents willing to make baptismal promises on a child's behalf, including raising that child in a Christian community of believers, it makes sense to delay the child's baptism until such promises are in place. Baptism is not magic. Saying so out loud may irk certain parishioners who've come to expect such family privileges.

"We know that we have passed from death to life because we love one another" (1 John 3:14). Baptism is a corporate gift with communal implications of love and service. I conclude this chapter with a wise shift in sacramental perspective offered by Paul Hoffman, whose faithful Seattle ministry—marked especially through presiding over and teaching about the historic catechumenate—has now shaped a generation of pastors in thinking about baptism in new and ancient ways:

> It is this care and thorough education around both baptism's gifts *and* its call to discipleship that builds a church for mission. It transforms the question of an egocentric generation from "What does baptism mean for me?" into "How does baptism initiate me into a life of service and compassion for others?" If the former is the only question upon which we are focused, is it any wonder that baptism is seen as a single moment in time in which each recipient of the sacrament becomes eternally cared for? When baptism is broadened to include that salvific gift *and* all of the disciplines that following Jesus offers us as

Christians, then baptism becomes a life-giving, lifelong journey of discovery.[30]

~~~~~~

I've covered quite a bit of ground in the first four chapters of this book, making a case that a return to parish-wide baptismal renewal is perhaps the central key to overcoming the paralyzing fear that often grips parishioners living in the early decades of the twenty-first century—a fear not unlike that revealed by the jailer who encountered Paul and Silas in Acts 16 prior to the jailer's baptism, or the fear of death that bound the community of Martha, Mary, and Lazarus in John 11.

Confronting the fear that gripped the disciples on the sea as they repeatedly traveled with Jesus to "the other side" is a central component of shaping faithful mission in any age. The radical baptismal claims found in Colossians ("you have died") and Romans 6 ("we have been buried with Christ by baptism into death") have great potential, therefore, in liberating any congregation for radical discipleship.

Any baptism celebrated in any century connects with the baptism of Jesus in this regard: we are greatly loved children of God—aggressively pursued, relentlessly tailed by goodness and mercy (Ps 23) on this side of the grave. Sunday preaching and pastoral care cannot return to these baptismal themes of origin and identity too often. An entire pastoral tenure could be shaped around such themes. Faithful baptismal practice will consistently revisit the biblical realities of dying and rising in planning appropriate celebrations to welcome new Christians into the body of Christ. We can learn from the unusual and life-giving practices of the early church in this regard.

An interlude is in order. Let's take a time-out and enter the parish customs and rhythms of a rural congregation and its pastor facing a variety of modern challenges. I offer the following short story to step back briefly from the theoretical to enter the rhythm of a fictional and flawed assembly of Christians (all of us, yes?), faithfully attempting ministry centered in baptismal promise. I'll offer poststory commentary in the book's closing chapter.

5

Interlude

~~~~~~

"DIGGING"

Cecil Graves slipped into four-wheel drive and crept into successive dark depths in the gravel road that almost swallowed his hubcaps. The pastor recalled failed petition attempts to pave the old trade route up Cedar Creek, used in one fashion or another for at least two hundred years, probably longer according to a part-Cherokee family who lived near the church. The ruts in the road, deep gashes in spots, needed more attention than the annual postwinter grading offered by the Watauga County DOT, especially following thunderstorms like the one that rattled through two nights ago.

"No way some of our older church members can come this way tomorrow morning," the pastor said over a low hint of the Saturday Sunrise Top 40 radio program on WUNC he somehow received all the way from Chapel Hill.

A large tree branch in the road, still barely attached to a dying adelgid-afflicted hemlock, failed to budge after Cecil exited the truck cab and tried to drag it out of the way. He drove around the blocked lane, the truck listing precipitously for a moment on the low side of the road. He'd send someone back down the mountain with a chain saw.

Cecil had the windows of his truck down on the mild May morning and heard a towhee to the left of his perched elbow on a smooth stretch of the road. He envisioned Carlene Townsend giving him an earful tomorrow at the church door because she had to come up the back way through Valle Crucis, adding an extra ten miles in both directions for worship she hadn't missed for a record number of Sundays.

Joe and Dickie Mendenhall were unloading their tools at the far end of the cemetery behind Saint Luke Lutheran Church as Cecil drove up. More church members—mostly guys from the property committee—would soon assemble on this fifth Saturday after Easter, but the pastor knew from a false early assumption in his ministry at Saint Luke that more than one woman in the congregation could swing a pretty mean pickax.

Cecil unlocked the back door of the fellowship hall to start the coffee and turned to wave at the two brothers across the distance that separated them, easily comprising three hundred headstones and grave markers, some dating back 150 years to the congregation's origins.

The pastor looked east and admired the sun just now topping the line of large oak trees on the near ridge. A church elder once told Cecil that chestnuts grew on the same ridge a hundred years ago, blighted wood now viewable in these mountains only via notched timbers grooved together in the cabins where some of his members were born and still reside.

~~~~~~

Cecil Graves learned of the church cemetery policy only after he arrived at Saint Luke; no one bothered to mention it during the call interviews. At first, the new pastor right out of seminary was enamored with the prohibition of backhoes on the property and a group effort to dig all graves by hand. It often gave him an extended chance to teach about baptism and dying and rising with Christ. Cecil laughed many times along with other church members at the ribbing he received from wordplay with his surname.

Digging a grave with seven or eight mourners—good friends of the deceased to be lowered two days hence into the rectangular hole—brought unusual benefits to the difficult labor. As he walked toward the Mendenhall brothers that morning after making coffee, Cecil recalled several of the many stories he always heard while taking his own turn with a shovel or pickax, often over his head below the grassy surface of the cemetery, sermon fodder he'd sometimes use for the funeral liturgy.

The grave digging also reminded him of his own baptism and how the watery union with Christ described in Romans 6 served to drive out fear and apprehension of the future. "Don't forget," he'd always tell the diggers. "We've already died." Cecil had been their pastor long enough that nobody had to ask what he meant. He did sometimes wonder if he was reassuring himself more than those who listened. Cecil probably worried more than most about changes coming to the mountains and what they meant for Saint Luke Church.

Church guidelines required an eight-foot depth for grave plots, deeper than most cemeteries. Sam Horton—a blacksmith now awaiting the Lord's call with his wife, Jeanette, under a headstone only twenty yards from this Saturday's dig site—once explained to Cecil that a deeper plot was "without question a *necessitary* in these old mountains due to all the rain we-uns get up he-ah."

The church still relied on spring water and an underground source that never ran dry, even in last summer's drought, so Cecil didn't doubt Sam's claim. The pastor also knew there was something powerful and faith-forming about looking up at cloud and sky from the bottom of a hole and hearing encouraging voices from the topside. Digging a grave also put the digger in touch with shared mortality and a future union with the saints gathered on a hill like this one. Baptism did indeed create a huge new family.

The whole process took most of a day, holy time to share common grief with sweat, tears, and laughter. Arrowheads, pieces of clay pots, and artifacts from another time were often discovered as the hole got deeper. Cecil once brought home the head of an old stone hatchet, now resting on his fireplace mantel, discovered at the four-foot mark of a grave for Orville Johnson (strongest tenor in the Saint Luke choir) after a terrible head-on accident on the Boone highway.

The digging ensemble usually took a break around noon for lunch, about halfway through the task. Cecil never asked about the origins of this part of the tradition, but he always loved the sacramental symbolism of sitting around the hole, passing around food, seven pairs of feet arranged in subterranean symmetry so close that everyone was linked by boot and jean.

As he walked toward Joe and Dickie that morning before the others arrived, Cecil again recalled how much he loved this congregation and the old ways of doing things. He also knew that it was getting increasingly difficult to locate seven strong backs willing to do such work on a Saturday morning. Before he greeted the two brothers with a thermos of hot coffee, the pastor tried to wipe away the image of a backhoe rumbling up the steep road along Cedar Creek.

"We were originally expecting four others in the next half hour, Pastor," said Dickie Mendenhall. "At least that's what my brother tells me. He was in charge of gathering the troops. I'm in charge of lunch."

Joe reddened a bit under his beard and App State ball cap. "Well, you might wish we'd have reversed the responsibilities, Cecil. I was eventually only able to corral Lukas Givens—plays linebacker for Foscoe High, ya know—and Mildred Blevins."

Cecil laughed at the two brothers even though he knew they'd all be digging until sundown. He always enjoyed how one brother called the pastor by his first name and the other persisted in a title, an old division of opinion in the Mendenhall family that stretched back to the brothers' grandparents, buried at the south end of the cemetery.

"So that makes only five of us? Including a teenager and an eighty-year-old woman? You better have some darn good vittles, boys."

"I think she's eighty-six, actually," said Joe. "Phoned me Thursday night to volunteer and told me so herself. I couldn't turn her down. Thought we might have plenty of help, but here we are. I think a lot of people are over on the parkway for some wildflower festival at Moses Cone Park. Lukas promised to swing by Mildred's place on the way up the mountain."

The shadow of a backhoe again lumbered across the pastor's mind. He looked up and saw a red-tailed hawk fly high over the church steeple.

Cecil knew Mildred dearly loved her second cousin, Roy Blevins, and would find special meaning in helping to dig his grave, but the pastor wondered how much help she'd be, an old woman who sometimes used a cane to get up the front steps of the church. He walked several paces away from the brothers and phoned his wife, Emma, telling her not to wait on dinner that evening.

~~~~~~

"Young man, I appreciate your kindness, but done told you once already I can make it just fine by myself. Been walkin' these hills and through these old tombstones since I was a little girl. Even remember crawlin' across this grassy knoll to look down in my own granddaddy's grave before we buried him. Momma says I plumb near fell in. I will take one of those shovels from the back of your Silverado when you get a chance."

Lukas Givens smiled, raising his eyebrows, as he looked over the passenger side door at the three men, suggesting without words that his time with Mildred Blevins that morning had already been something of an adventure. A junior at the high school, Lukas was one of several teenagers (like Cecil's own two sons, ten years previous) in the congregation who would attend college far from the shadow of Grandfather Mountain and never return except for holidays. Lukas was athletic with good grades, an Eagle Scout, exceptionally polite.

"Yes, ma'am, you did tell me. I apologize. Won't happen again."

Cecil asked everyone to gather around the site of the Blevins family plot where the digging would soon commence. The pastor glanced at his watch: 7:34. He thanked the four parishioners for taking time to help. They all bowed their heads.

"Lord, we give you thanks for Roy's life. A good man, faithful and flawed like any of us. We recall good times and sad with those who've gone before us on this mountain, knowing that you've accompanied us every step of the way. Guide our hearts and hands this day as we work together and turn soil that birthed and feeds your people. Remind us of our common baptism that indeed prepares us all for that day when we're joined with the saints forever. Amen."

"And just how was he flawed?" Mildred asked her pastor across the small circle of joined hands.

Cecil pretended to look confused.

"My cousin, Roy. One of the best men ever born in these parts. Tell me his faults."

"I wasn't thinking anything specific, Mildred," said the pastor as memories of Roy's serial marital infidelities raced across his imagination. "You know how we say in the confession that we're all 'in bondage to sin and cannot free ourselves.' Right out of First John. That's what I meant."

Without responding, Mildred reached back to locate the long shovel that had been leaning between her bony shoulder blades, raised it slightly above the crown of long black hair wrapped in a red bandanna, and sunk the point four inches into the soil, barely missing her pastor's right boot.

"And we're off!" Joe shouted, raising his ball cap to the sky then pulling it low over his eyes.

The four men walked to the two trucks to retrieve tools. "Nice postprayer recovery, Pastor," whispered Dickie.

~~~~~~

They made better time than Cecil predicted. By ten o'clock, the five of them, taking turns, had removed close to three feet of soil and packed clay with impressive rectangular precision. Mildred's strength and stamina were something of a surprise. Joe was particularly adept at carving the beginning of smooth walls on the four sides of the grave.

"Gotta get 'em straight early on or you'll regret it later. I recall one funeral—you remember, Cecil—for old Troy Turbeville. The hole was plenty deep enough. But when the pallbearers started to lower Troy on down, he only made it halfway, completely stuck. We had to change into work clothes after everybody went home and dug a couple more hours. Lukas, your uncle Ronnie—what's he weigh these days, about three hundred?—even tried to jump on top of Troy's casket, but the poor guy just wouldn't budge. It was a heck of an operation getting him out of the hole to resume digging. Ropes, mighty grunts, cussin'. Forgive me, Lord. Naw, I learned that day to get the walls straight."

The men took a water break, leaning against the trucks. Mildred shook her head when offered a cup and spread a frayed Star of Bethlehem quilt near her grandfather's grave. It was getting warm. She stretched out, removed work gloves, locked her fingers behind her head, and looked up at the sky, soon humming the tune to "Come, Thou Fount."

"I love that hymn," Cecil said. "A fine baptism hymn."

"Aren't pastors supposed to love 'em all?" Mildred said in the direction of an overhead cloud. It was the first words she'd spoken since the opening prayer.

The pastor caught the eyes of the brothers, grinned, and shook his head.

"Hot, isn't it? For mid-May anyway," Lukas said. He removed his varsity hoodie. The men laughed at the T-shirt underneath and the teenager quickly donned the garment he'd just removed.

"Please share the amusement, Lukas Givens," Mildred said, still looking up. "I wasn't born yesterday."

Lukas finally gave in after several unsuccessful attempts at distraction.

"I forgot I was wearing it—not something I should have in my wardrobe anyway. The T-shirt's a statement about that condo on the other side of Grandfather. The one that rises up ten stories above the ridge and you can see all the way from Banner Elk?"

Mildred laughed for the first time that day. "You mean the condo our very own pastor said was like 'a giant finger stuck up in the face of God'? I doubt you know that very comment made the front page of the *Winston-Salem Journal* about ten years ago, when you were a second-grader."

Lukas didn't say so, but he did know.

"Let's have a look, young man."

The three men tried to squelch laughter. Dickie gave Lukas a push. The teenager reddened and trudged over to the woman five times his age as if he were walking a plank. He again removed the hoodie. Mildred sat up and fished glasses from a hidden pouch in her jacket.

She slowly took in the T-shirt's meaning. A clenched fist of angry protest. A raised middle finger painted as an admirably close facsimile of the condo. The words "A View from Heaven," arranged in a frown.

"Well, I never . . ." said the old woman, smiling.

Before she could complete the sentence, something whirring and mechanical—the size of a hawk—dropped out of the sky and almost hit Pastor Cecil Graves in the head.

~~~~~~

Cecil grew up loving mountains. His grandparents lived near Asheville, and the trip over from Tennessee to see them included several winding miles along the Ocoee River near Copper Hill, south of the Smokies. Cecil could look out the back seat window with his two brothers and see the slatted walls of a log flume hugging the side of the mountain far above the streambed, almost blending into the contours of the shadowed slope. Cecil wondered about the hidden timber that floated mysteriously to a lumber mill downstream. He read books about how people made a living in landscapes where job possibilities didn't seem all that obvious. The little boy once saw a congregation of people out of the car window, with a smaller group all in white, gathering on the near bank of the Ocoee. His father slowed the car out of respect and said a mass baptism was about to occur. "Baptism is the most important date in anybody's life," his dad explained. "But in these mountains especially, it links people together and gives them hope in an uncertain future." Cecil remembered looking back, upstream, and seeing a girl about his age go under.

Emma and Cecil Graves decided early in their years at seminary to love a congregation nobody much wanted. Their time at Saint Luke included several pay cuts for Cecil not because of poor pastoral performance but due to a church census that continued to shrink despite his best efforts. Emma found a job as a teacher's aide when their boys started first grade. The Graves family somehow made it on two skinny salaries and a lot of garden produce.

The pastor watched old people die and young people leave the mountains for jobs in Hickory and Greensboro. With each burial, it seemed Cecil was observing a way of life slowly slip away. He stopped counting the number of real estate agents who'd made lucrative offers for the church property.

It was tempting for a landowner to sell out. County legal codes often benefited new developers. Ski resorts were an economic boon to the tax base in the eyes of the elected. For most of Cecil's older parishioners, homesteads that had been in families for generations were slowly taxed for their potential use based on the land value of a nearby resort. It became difficult to fight and stay. A massive clear-cut, barely out of view across the ridge from the church cemetery, would soon accommodate seven new slopes, noisy all-night snowblowers, thirty vacation rentals, and who knew what else.

Several in the congregation welcomed the changes and the needed jobs brought by such developments to the western part of the county. *Sustainability* was a word that academics over at the university used, an idea Cecil quickly learned would never fly in a sermon. Fast cash made a lot more sense to many than no cash at all. Saint Luke's pristine setting and tradition seemed surrounded at times by encroaching noise and unceasing night glow from nearby lights. Emma and Cecil had lingered in the parking lot after Christmas Eve service the December before Roy Blevins died. Emma stated that night what her husband had already observed many times after late evening meetings: "Ever notice how the star-show up here has changed since we arrived twenty years ago?"

There were holdouts, no doubt—people like the Mendenhall brothers, the sprawling Blevins clan, and the Townsend family, still thirty members strong in Saint Luke's pews. At one time, those three names alone owned much of the land bordering Cedar Creek as it tumbled down the mountain toward Foscoe. They could afford to resist a long time if necessary.

More than once, Cecil had to vouch for a church member whose buckshot whizzed a little too close to a real estate agent making the mistake of parking on private property. The pastor knew that one of Mildred's brothers, Larry, kept a loaded shotgun leaning near the front door of his cabin. Cecil wondered more than once how a man in a wheelchair could aim the thing, but he had to admire the old man's spirit. Larry, like many of his parishioners, seemed fearless. "I'm baptized, ain't I?" Larry asked his pastor.

~~~~~~

"It's one of them *crones*, ain't it?" Mildred hollered back, too far out of earshot to hear the four males chuckling at the apt rhyme. "I seen about them flyin' varmints on Fox the other night. They spy on people."

The old woman had leaped to her feet from the quilt quicker than Cecil thought possible. She was rummaging through red bee balm at the far side of the cemetery, poking near the fallen object with her shovel. Two hummingbirds, first arrivers of the season, played tag around Mildred's head, intrigued by her bandanna's vivid kinship to the blossoms, darting for quick sips from the fragile flowers.

"Ms. Blevins, don't touch it," said Lukas, now by her side. "My friend Robert owns a smaller version of this drone—loses his all the time. There might be a way to return this one to its owner, but I'd leave it alone for now. We might need to report it to the police."

"The dang thing's squirmin' and buzzin' like a wounded animal. I'm fixin' to put this un out of its mis-ry."

"Wouldn't surprise me at all, Pastor," said Dickie Mendenhall, "if this flying intruder is scoping out church property for Randy Real Estate. I always thought their last name perfectly matched the whole sordid enterprise. I wonder if we can take us a little peek at the photo footage attached to this contraption."

"Cecil," Joe chimed in, "since this one's not a quad but rather an octocopter, eight propellers and all, I suspect the five of us may be on *Candid Camera* even as we speak—at least that's what my buddy Earl tells me. That is, unless the batteries are dead, but Mildred's right. The thing's still buzzin' louder than these hummers, all excited to get drunk on bee balm nectar like some avian New Year's Eve. I think we should all wave back at the owner."

"I ain't wavin' at nobody," said Mildred, who again raised the shovel far above her sweaty bandanna and started a forceful downward plunge toward the flashing machine that instead (this time) barely missed the pastor's left boot.

Cecil briefly wondered who was indeed on trial. "Whoa now," he said. "Let's hold up a minute."

"There's a good chance," said Lukas, "that the owner knows about the crash, the drone's location, and may be on the way up here to retrieve it. I think we should just leave it alone for a while. I've got a date tonight and we've got a good bit of shoveling left, not to mention a lunch break. If nobody shows up before we finish digging Roy's grave, we can make some decisions then."

"Now that's a wise young man," said the pastor. "No wonder you're already an Eagle Scout, Lukas. OK with you two brothers? OK with you, Mildred?"

The old woman grunted an assent and feigned a shovel-prod at the still buzzing machine. She loosened the bandanna from her brow and tied a ponytail knot in her long hair, surprisingly just starting to silver.

The five church members used their shovels like walking staffs, making their way back to the grave and the growing mound of loose earth. Mildred stopped every few steps and looked back toward the bee balm and the hummingbirds. Her pose reminded Cecil of Lot's wife and the sad pillar of salt, even though Mildred gazed at the fallen drone with suspicion rather than longing. Or maybe it was a little of both. They passed around spring water under the rising sun and resumed digging.

〜〜〜〜〜

Cecil was surprised a woman of Mildred's age and countenance owned a pair of Hi-Tec hiking shoes with purple laces, but there they were, dangling in Roy Blevins's grave alongside eight worn work boots as Dickie Mendenhall unloaded lunch from a small cooler he'd retrieved from the back of his truck.

"Pastor," said Dickie. "I knew from past potlucks here at Saint Luke that you're partial to chicken salad and barbecue chips. Hope that's OK with everybody."

Dickie passed out the sandwiches—white bread, plenty of mayo. The brothers sat on one long side of the grave. Cecil and Lukas sat opposite. Mildred took up residence on the high end, where her cousin's head would soon rest. She had a straight view toward the occasional buzz and whir still faintly emanating from the distant bee balm. Her red bandanna and long hair fluttered a bit in a gentle wind that normally kicked up in the early afternoon on a sunny day. It was now nearing 1:00 p.m. Cecil led the group in a short prayer thanking the Lord for land and larder.

"I guess it's usually *the pastor* that gets to decide everything around here from menu to moonshine," Mildred muttered, just loud enough to be heard.

The brothers looked at Cecil with raised eyebrows and wondered if Lukas had also somehow heard about the snort passed around under a full moon between Pastor Graves and the property committee guys after their April meeting. The teenager shooed mock judgment toward each guilty man—Lukas's right index finger silently moving across his left pointer.

Mildred laughed. She missed nothing. "Confession is good for the soul, gentlemen!"

For a distraction and to honor the tradition, Cecil asked the four diggers if they'd like to share any stories about Roy. "The funeral is Monday at four," he reminded them. "Hope you can all make it. Lukas, I know you probably have track practice, but maybe Coach Jones will understand."

They took turns talking, chewing chicken salad.

Lukas told a story about how Roy once got the youth group nearly lost on a hike up Grandfather. "We got back to the trailhead after dark with one flashlight."

"Roy was always the first to volunteer to take the bread and wine from Sunday worship to homebound church members," Cecil offered. The pastor couldn't resist a short homily about how any shared food—including chicken salad sandwiches—was eucharistic in nature, recalling the promised presence of Jesus when "two or more, let's say five, are gathered."

"He became something of a surrogate father when our dad died," Joe said. "We weren't even teenagers, Cecil; needed an older male influence. He picked us up, took us to Mountaineer football games in Boone. Carried us to Scout meetings, all sorts of places. I know some people said he had a few flaws; we all do. But that man was a godsend to two young boys. He faithfully lived out his baptism, that's for sure."

"*Who said he had flaws?!*" Mildred brayed across the hole, rearing back a ponytailed head. Like an indignant prophetess, she simultaneously engaged a right Hi-Tec with her pastor's left shin.

"Not an accident," Cecil told Emma later that night as she examined the raised bruise.

"Tell me again why you feel a need to tell stories with your feet in a grave?" Emma asked.

~~~~~

Cecil was alone in the church office early Monday morning, putting the last touches on Roy's funeral bulletin. Due to recent budget cuts, he'd taken over some of the secretarial duties but really didn't mind coming in. He loved the silence and solitude of the church property on a weekday. The mountain would be full of mourners and old friends soon enough. Cecil heard several towhees calling *"Drink your tea"* back and forth in the laurel outside the window. He raised his cup to them and listened for a while to Cedar Creek, which gurgled over ancient stones below the church building.

The pastor ignored the first round of telephone rings but figured he'd better answer after a second call commenced ten seconds later.

"Pastor Graves, this is Officer Blake Holmes from Sheriff Blake's office."

Cecil briefly pondered the odd coincidence of name synchronicity.

"I serve on the county narcotics investigation team," Officer Holmes continued. "One of our drones went down over the weekend and the memory chip keeps pinging back signals to my phone. Our octocopter is either on or very near your church property. Haven't seen it, have you?"

Cecil quickly thought back to late Saturday, the last shovelful of earth extracted from Roy's grave, and the group decision to leave the drone alone in the protective cover of bee balm to see if an owner might drive up the mountain to claim it.

"Yes, 'bout hit me in the head around lunch on Saturday during a workday. We decided to leave it be. I was gonna call the police department this morning if nobody came around to claim the thing," Cecil said, truthfully, "but noticed after church yesterday that it was gone. It landed on the far side of our cemetery in some tall grass, spring flowers."

"Y'all are the church where members still dig the graves for the deceased, aren't you?"

"Yes sir, that's us. We have a funeral service this afternoon, and that's what five of us were doing Saturday."

"I think that's pretty amazing and admirable. An old-time tradition in these parts that you hardly ever see anymore. I take my hat off to you. I heard about Roy. Fine man."

"I should have called you earlier," Cecil said.

"Don't worry about that, Pastor. You'll read about this in the paper, though, so I'll tell you now. That drone was scoping out a suspected hidden pot farm not far from your church. Sometimes the operational signal goes haywire and we lose one."

"We noticed it was still making noises."

"Yeah, that's how I knew to call you. We have enough evidence, as it turns out, without the drone footage. Listen, I also need to tell you—you'll read about this, too—that we have a young man in custody, a great-nephew of one of your older members, in connection with the drug bust. Actually, also related to the man you'll bury this afternoon. Danny Blevins? Does that name ring a bell?"

***

Before they processed to the cemetery in a warm, overcast mist that afternoon, the gathered congregation sang "There's a Wideness in God's Mercy" for the closing hymn, even though Cecil was pretty sure Mildred wouldn't like it.

"It fits Roy," Cecil had told Emma over a late lunch in the faculty lounge of her school. "Heck, it fits any of us; fits me."

The hymn concluded as Cecil reached the front steps of the church. He noticed the parking lot was full—impressive given the condition of Cedar Creek Road—as he followed the crucifer out of the church and into the cemetery along a path of artfully arranged stones. The pastor thought, "Here's one thing mountain people will never relinquish to a fading past: honoring the dead. Honoring baptism, really."

A few umbrellas came out as mourners carefully followed the cross. Lukas Givens's girlfriend, Molly, heading to Chapel Hill in the fall to study music, offered a slow fiddle tune, "Ashokan Farewell." Canes steadied aging hips and legs. Elbows and arms found support from younger hands.

At least one hundred people, most of the congregation that had assembled inside, gathered around Roy's grave. The sun briefly broke through. Cecil heard an older man in the back of the crowd say much louder than intended, "The devil's beatin' his wife."

The pastor read from Ezekiel 37, describing a valley of dry bones and God's promise to "open your graves" and bring the Lord's people to a new land. He offered prayers, which included a remembrance of baptism and a slow pouring of ample spring water into the open grave. Cecil recited a commendation and committal that Saint Luke members knew by heart. As Roy's coffin was lowered into the earth, a deep and sonorous hand-bell rang twelve times, signifying his place as a disciple of Jesus. Three verses of "Amazing Grace" rang across the cemetery with boldness and clarity.

Cecil always loved what came next, the completion of an old tradition. Anyone who wished to remain could take turns spading earth back in place with three long shovels waiting upright, jabbed into the mound of dirt—always three. Cecil wasn't sure if the tradition might be a commentary on the Holy Trinity. From a distance, on the walk from the church, the upright shovel handles reminded him of the two thieves alongside Jesus on the cross.

About fifteen people remained to start the shoveling process while the rest of the crowd walked back toward the fellowship hall for refreshments.

The faithful diggers of any Saint Luke grave always shoveled first. Lukas, Joe, and Dickie each took a turn. Mildred paused at the edge of her cousin's grave, looking down, Cecil thought, upon all the shared years.

The old woman threw in more shovels-full of earth than her pastor thought possible. She handed Cecil her shovel as others grabbed the remaining two from the mound. Together at the head of the grave, Mildred caught her pastor's eye and held the look for a few moments, a beat longer than felt comfortable.

He thought she was about to say something, but Mildred only offered a hint of the satisfied smile the pastor had seen many times before. She made the sign of the cross across her chest and nodded.

Cecil would later tell Emma that he swore he heard a muffled buzz and whir from somewhere eight feet below.

6
Casting Out Fear
Every Sunday

I lost all sense of fear. When you lose your sense of fear, you're free.

—Congressman John Lewis (1940–2020)

True courage is not denial of risk; it is mastery of fear when risk must be judiciously confronted to serve a higher (usually unselfish) goal. Courage requires focusing on others, rather than on yourself, and is, as a bonus, among the best ways to manage fear.

—Abigail Marsh

The Lord is my light and my salvation;
  whom shall I fear?
The Lord is the stronghold of my life;
  of whom shall I be afraid?

—Psalm 27:1

Fear potentially paralyzes any congregation—fear from the guilt of past mistakes and words that still linger and wound; fear of encroaching change that threatens a shared history, often idealistically recalled through a revisionist lens; fear of social and political forces that seek to splinter faith communities along partisan divides encompassing lesser identities (compared to the ancient strength of baptism), including family, party, gender, sexuality, and race; fear of a future that includes the looming reality of death and earthly finitude.

The characters and details of "Digging" are an attempt to examine several fears in one southern Appalachian mountain congregation. The narrative I shaped is entirely fictional. The setting, however, and the cemetery custom of shared grave digging are based on my seminary internship congregation near Boone, North Carolina. I've been over my head in a grave in that cemetery, digging and telling stories about the deceased, a rather poignant subterranean perspective from which to ponder a shared future and the radical promises of God. The massive changes in those mountains in the last fifty years, largely brought by tourism and the snow ski industry, are somewhat unique to that setting. Any congregation, however, will need to engage in their own holy act of digging to unearth powerful aspects of the past that will instill courage for current challenges and unite a body of people for whom fear of the future is brought into proper sacramental focus. Having crossed the baptismal sea, the resurrection light of Christ goes before his people like the ancient pillar of fire, leading us on in trust and hope from place to place and moment to moment, overcoming any spiritual thirst (Meribah) or hunger (Manna) along the way. Baptism, faithfully understood and celebrated, creates a new people liberated from the fear of death.

Martin Luther undoubtedly stressed the daily remembrance of one's baptism because he knew of the many fear-inducing incidents numbing any group of Christians planted in any community in any decade. This is an audacious baptismal confession to offer aloud, with Saint Paul: "I have been crucified with

Christ; and it is no longer I who live, but it is Christ who lives in me" (Gal 2:19–20).

I have already died in baptism; it can be dated—July 28, 1957.

There is something about saying that (and truly believing it) that is immensely helpful and hopeful in moving through any day, regardless of the challenges the day brings. We are freed to celebrate the wonder of life, the intricate, mysterious gifts of creation, and the variety of personalities in our churches and communities whose opinions and convictions may not match our own but who've been brought by God into our intersecting paths as neighbors to engage and love. Confessing that we've died in baptism gives Christians (who may differ with one another on a constellation of social issues) a pretty amazing place to start and find common ground. I'm convinced that such a vision gave Christian leaders like John Lewis creative courage to take another step toward what Christ had in mind for his beloved community. Reflecting upon baptism, even an enemy became worthy of radical love. Civil rights leader Will Campbell (1924–2013) angered not a few friends when he dared to attend Klan meetings in the South to share the radical love of the Lord: "We did not understand that those we so vulgarly called 'redneck' were a part of the tragedy."[1] A remarkable and liberating statement to confess aloud.

As congregations dig into a liturgical past for meaning and hope, perhaps this recovery of sacramental death is the very thing to shake us all free from the paralyzing fear that grips us, so masterfully exploited at times by our national political leaders. To confess this truth daily could undoubtedly change a lot: *I have already died; nothing out there can "get" me; God has freed me to love and live without fear.*

E. L. Doctorow once observed, "Writing a novel is like driving a car at night. You can only see as far as your headlights, but you can make the whole trip that way."[2] This same insight can be applied to the baptismal confession that serves as the central thesis for this book. Regularly claiming the truth and promise of dying with Christ in baptism surprisingly drives away darkness and provides light for the next steps on the journey. "Your word is a lamp to my feet and a light to my path" (Ps 119:105); there's a sense of incremental trust conveyed in this famous verse. Ditto for dying in baptism. If this is the church's common sacramental identity, we together "can make the whole trip" in such confident fashion, one step at a time down the winding path, "always carrying in the body the death of Jesus, so that the life of Jesus may also be made visible in our bodies" (2 Cor 4:10).

I'm writing these words just after my wife, Cindy, and I have come through the slog of positive testing for the coronavirus. My case was uncomfortable but fairly mild; hers pretty serious. The fourteen-day quarantine (day three coincided with our thirty-ninth wedding anniversary) gave us plenty of time to read, think, and pray together. I was struck during this period by an article in *National Geographic*, written by a Princeton philosophy major, Oliver Whang, whose education was interrupted by the pandemic, resulting in an unplanned return to his childhood home, living with his parents:

> For many young people like me—with healthy bodies and outsize beliefs of invincibility—the primary fear hasn't been that we will contract the virus. What we fear more is the profound uncertainty of our future. There are a lot of frightening possibilities; new ones seem to emerge every day. But I think the scariest possibility—beyond this disease never going away—is that this ubiquity of virtual living might never go away either. I worry that the experience of this pandemic might convince people that we can keep living just fine while physically isolated from others.[3]

How might the promise of baptism address such a poignantly stated fear of the future, an apprehension not far removed from the concerns of countless congregations and their pastors who've relied on the gift and limitations of virtual worship to try to build community during the pandemic?

A couple weeks after our symptoms subsided, Cindy and I journeyed for a delayed anniversary celebration to an old inn situated on the Blue Ridge Parkway near Mount Pisgah (elevation 5,722 feet) above Asheville, North Carolina, complete with social distancing etiquette, summer highs that rarely leave the low seventies, and a great restaurant with masked servers. Over five feet of snow once fell on this southern mountain in a freakish two-day storm in early May of 1992, trapping guests at the inn. A short hike to nearby Fryingpan Lookout Tower offers stunning views in all directions. We climbed several sets of stairs, clung to the uppermost railing, and looked back toward Mount Pisgah on a cloudless morning.

In the thirty-fourth and final chapter of the book of Deuteronomy, Moses hikes from the plains of Moab to the summit of Mount Pisgah (the North Carolina peak we were viewing from the fire tower takes its name from this story) and looks upon the panoramic span of the promised land toward which the veteran leader has been leading a stubborn people all these years. The Lord accompanies Moses on his hike and speaks: "This is the land of which I swore to Abraham, to Isaac, and to Jacob, saying, 'I will give it to your descendants'; I have let you see it with your eyes, but you shall not cross over there" (Deut 34:4). It's tempting to get derailed here and focus upon Moses's forbidden entrance into the land, stemming from what seems to be a rather minor misunderstanding (see Num 20:12) with God. The resulting divine prohibition still leaves scholars scratching their heads. Moses is given only a glimpse, a fleeting taste of what's ahead for his people from a forty-year body of work. Hardly seems fair.

I'll try not to push the analogy too far here, but Moses's long, circuitous toiling in the wilderness is similar to the labors of any faithful pastor who leads his or her flock weekly. Pastors help enlist followers of Jesus who are dunked into a new reality, crossing a sacramental sea toward the other side, and aligning with a faithful yet flawed (and sometimes complaining) body of people traveling together on a long journey. Pastors place bread in the palms of their parishioners, "a foretaste of the feast to come,"[4] sometimes summoning a reaction similar to our spiritual forebears in the wilderness who gathered manna, a Hebrew word that literally means, "What is it?" A Christian crowd of impatient sojourners might ask, "Don't we need a bit more sustenance and nourishment for these arduous days than a nibble of bread and sip of wine?" With Moses, we receive a peek from the peak of Sunday worship, depart into a world of suffering and challenge, and return the following Sunday for another shared glimpse toward the promised land up ahead. Is it enough?

I don't know whether Oliver Whang's anxiety concerning sustained viral isolation is also tinged with theological regret and personal ecclesial rejection. If his anxiety matches that of many young adults of my acquaintance (including my three children), I'd say theology (and its perceived limitations) is indeed part of the mix. If baptism is simply a way to get one's ticket punched for future entrance into a promised land in the sweet by and by, then a rejection of the church's promises is perhaps warranted. Parish recovery of baptism as sacramental death, however, resulting in an identity that radically unites the baptized with Christ in the here and now may be just the theological pivot needed to address the isolation created by a pandemic. A community that regularly recalls and announces that they've already died has nothing to fear; we are oddly united by the very thing that humans tend to fear the most. From this perspective, not only is the church given a glimpse of the land ahead, but the beloved community has together already entered it.

Perhaps pastoral proclamation should consistently keep in mind the odd story of Balaam and his talking donkey, a tale that commences only two chapters later in Numbers after Moses's slipup resulting in promised land prohibition. The story is usually remembered for a verbal burro and sword-wielding angel who both finally convince Balaam that his powers of prophecy are best offered in service to God rather than the behest of a partisan power and the king of Moab's royal finger-snapping summons, beseeching a favorable future. (Please recall that any pastor is centrally answerable to God rather than any congregation's power contingent; surely you've noticed such power exists.) Standing before King Balak of Moab, who is not happy with an underling's tardy delay in answering the royal summons, Balaam, our reluctant hero, offers a zinger any preacher might wisely memorize: "I have come to you now, but do I have the power to say just anything? The word God puts in my mouth, that is what I must say" (Num 22:38).

Balaam then proceeds to deliver a series of four pointed oracles that serve to royally tick off a king who thought he had another sycophantic prophet in his back pocket. My favorite is the fourth oracle. Balaam, the flawed and once-reluctant prophet whose rear end was saved by his talking ass, has come full circle in his devotion to God's guiding: "The oracle of one who hears the words of God, and knows the knowledge of the Most High, who sees the vision of the Almighty, who falls down, but with his eyes uncovered" (24:16).

What a marvelous metaphor for any flawed but faithful pastor. *One who falls down with uncovered eyes!* Of course, there will be setbacks and disappointments in the pastoral life, complete with falls, stumbling, and mistakes. But the faithful pastor stumbles with eyes wide open on the way down, the ministerial gaze fixed solely upon the Lord God's divine and often circuitous guidance: "Remember the long way that the Lord your God has led you these forty years" (Deut 8:2). Express insight is rather rare.

A strong hunch—it's the pattern of baptismal dying and rising (radically shaping the pastoral identity) that provides courage and chutzpah for any pastor to rise from the dust of disappointment and dare once again, with clear and uncovered eyes, to speak for God. "Our prayers break on God like waves," writes Luci Shaw in one of her poems, "and he an endless shore."[5] Sermons and other pastoral acts often resemble prayers repeatedly addressed to God in weekly waves guided by the recurring liturgical tide of the church year. Offered without clear clergy identity and purpose, these liturgical offerings can subtly wear upon pastors called to lead diverse and sometimes stubborn bodies of people.

"In my experience," wrote James Baldwin, for a while a teenage preacher in Harlem in the late 1930s, "the minister and his flock mirror each other. It demands a very rare, intrepid, and genuinely free and loving shepherd to challenge the habits and fears and assumptions of his flock and help them enter the freedom that enables us to move to higher ground. I was not that shepherd. And rather than betray the ministry, I left it."[6]

I suspect all pastors have felt the siren call to cease leading a congregation and find another vocation. That was certainly true for me in my thirty-one years on the job. It's tempting to serve as the "family preacher" who tries to make everyone happy with snippets of divine insight, summoned, running hither and yon to provide a bit of God on demand. (King Balak lives.) It's easy to confuse exactly who pastors are called to serve. A preacher's primary ordination, after all, is baptism, our watery death in Christ. Reborn, clear-eyed like reluctant Balaam, pastors are freed to speak for God without fear. When it becomes clear who we are truly called to serve, the "free and loving shepherd" is liberated to indeed challenge fear and lead a flock to higher ground.

～～～～～

There is a long, steep hill not far from our house in upstate South Carolina that climbs toward the local middle school sitting solidly atop the rise. I conclude daily bicycle rides with a slow ascent of this hill, attempting to keep in shape for longer tours on the bike, complete with panniers and camping gear. As I write these words, an adventure with an old seminary friend down the spine of the southern Appalachians along the length of the Blue Ridge Parkway is three weeks away. Those mountains will dwarf my nearby neighborhood hill and tax most any sixty-three-year-old posterior, including mine. These rehearsal rides are important. Only an insane cyclist would try to tackle the parkway without preliminary hill work.

The middle school hill rises past a soccer field and climbs toward a hilltop basketball court. Afternoons, courtside, there is often a passel of teenage boys from an outdoor gym class, preening and showing off for girls who are doing a poor job of pretending to ignore them. Sometimes the guys call out to the guy on the bicycle, puffing up the hill. I occasionally wave. The other day, an impudent adolescent swished an impressive jump shot from thirty feet, crashed into his pal with a sternum bump, and then called toward the road, "Hey, old man! You want a piece of me?"

I love Psalm 139: "You have searched me and known me. You discern my thoughts from far away." The psalm turns rather vindictive there at the end. I used to delete the vengeful part at funerals, but maybe it would have been OK to read the whole honest shebang. The psalms as a corpus are marvelous, transparent prayers that let God know what God already knows about us: that we are flawed creatures full of a messy stew of dark emotions. Even the best among us are odd works in progress when all the facades are peeled back.

God, I'm quite sure, knew that I wanted to climb out of my bike saddle that day, stride over to the basketball court, and take down Mr. Impudence in a quick game of one-on-one. Most of me really didn't want to do that, but my small adolescent self would've enjoyed the moment, even if I'd lost. "You . . . are acquainted with all my ways" (Ps 139:3). It depends on the day whether I find that statement terrifying or comforting. It's sometimes rather daunting to be known so completely; rather stunning that God loves me in spite of such intimate acquaintance.

"The cadences of worship," writes James K. A. Smith in his excellent book on Saint Augustine, "are the rhythms where we learn to be free. Freedom takes practice. . . . The point of the sacraments is that they are embodied conduits of grace that nourish new habits."[7] Baptism is a one-time dunking with daily implications for ongoing conversion. In remembrance of his baptism, Martin Luther made the sign of the cross the first thing in the morning before his feet hit the floor and then signed his tired body with the cross as his last conscious act before closing his eyes for sleep—a day bracketed with his own sacramental dying and rising. I am immensely thankful for Jesus, a Lord who waits patiently as I learn new habits over the length of days.

The baptismal paradigm shift I've described in this book cannot happen all at once in parish life. We have already died with Christ, swimming around in his grace this side of the grave. Confessing and believing such truth matters greatly. Creative proclamation and teaching in this regard are vital to congregational health. But like any shift in primary identity, the gift and work of conversion requires time and pastoral patience. The church has been immersed in very old and nourishing waters. The church, in its variety of global expressions, also lives daily alongside the reality of toxic fear. A Black pastor friend once confided that he never apologized for the length of Sunday worship services, usually three hours or more in his tradition: "For an entire six days, in so many ways, my people hear cultural voices telling them they're nobody and to be afraid. I need at least three hours on the seventh day to tell them they're somebody and to fear not."

I return to the opening of this book for a passage from C. S. Lewis's adventures in Narnia, *The Voyage of the Dawn Treader*, describing a young boy whose ornery behavior turned him into a scaly dragon. "The very first tear he made was so deep," said Eustace, speaking of Aslan, "that I thought it had gone right to my heart. And when he began pulling the skin off, it hurt worse than anything I've ever felt. Then he caught hold of me and threw me into the water. I'd turned into a boy again."

We've died in baptism. Christ goes straight for our hearts, mine prone to flirt with an ancient garden tree. Paraphrasing Luther, the old Adam is a pretty decent swimmer. Scales are removed. They grow back this side of the grave. Conversion is always an unfinished process with multiple transformations.

Dying, we rise. And rise again. And again.

Offering thanks and praise for the ancient cruciform tree of surpassing power and grace.

Notes

Introduction

Portions of this introduction are copyright © 2019 by the *Christian Century*. "Buried with Christ: Baptism Is about Dying" by Frank G. Honeycutt. It first appeared in and is reprinted with permission from the August 14, 2019, issue of the *Christian Century*, 26–29.

1 C. S. Lewis, *The Voyage of the Dawn Treader* (New York: Macmillan, 1952), 90.
2 Much of North American Protestantism inherited small baptismal font dimensions from European forebears. The difficulty of heating large worship spaces (and the danger of full immersion in winter months) led to the visual loss of the image of death in Christ by drowning.
3 I'm indebted to John Westerhoff for this story. See Westerhoff, *Bringing Up Children in the Christian Faith* (Minneapolis: Winston, 1980), 3.
4 El Salvador (where one of my daughters was born) remains one of Central America's most violent regions. See Jason Motlagh, "No Way Out," *National Geographic*, March 2019, 76–99.
5 Kathleen Norris, *The Cloister Walk* (New York: Riverhead, 1996), 204.
6 Gabe Huck, *How Can I Keep from Singing? Thoughts about Liturgy for Musicians* (Chicago: Liturgy Training, 1989), 24.

7 See, for example, John Fea, *Believe Me: The Evangelical Road to Donald Trump* (Grand Rapids, MI: Eerdmans, 2018).

8 Alice McDermott, *The Ninth Hour* (New York: Farrar, Straus and Giroux, 2017), 233.

Chapter 1

1 The bishop insisted upon the truth and authenticity of this story. The tale still packs a punch even if apocryphal. All names in this story are fabricated.

2 Flannery O'Connor, "The River," in *The Complete Stories* (New York: Farrar, Straus and Giroux, 1984), 168.

3 See especially Sally Fitzgerald, ed., *The Habit of Being: Letters of Flannery O'Connor* (New York: Vintage, 1980).

4 Flannery O'Connor, "The Fiction Writer and His Country," in *Literature for Composition: Essays, Fiction, Poetry, and Drama*, ed. Sylvan Barnet et al. (Upper Saddle River, NJ: Prentice Hall, 2000), 1254.

5 Literally, in the Greek, "a spirit of the Python." Afraid of snakes? This may be your liberation story.

6 They remind me of the Salvadoran woman mentioned in the introduction, countless plantation slaves who somehow managed to sing under persecution, and civil rights workers whose beatings and threats were punctuated with hymns.

7 Reminiscent of the blood and water (the fearless promise of baptism coupled with the reality of suffering) flowing from the side of Jesus on the cross in John 19:34.

8 Either the jailer lives inside the prison with his family or the trio departs for a few hours to find refreshment in the jailer's nearby kitchen before again returning. Take your pick. Both possibilities suggest the newfound chutzpah of this man who almost ended his life in quaking fear, no pun intended.

9 Steven Pinker, *The Better Angels of Our Nature: Why Violence Has Declined* (New York: Viking, 2011), esp. 1–30; Jack Hartnell, *Medieval Bodies: Life and Death in the Middle Ages* (New York: W. W Norton, 2018); and Geraldine Brooks, *Year of Wonders: A Novel of the Plague* (New York: Penguin, 2001). In this historical novel, Brooks focuses on the plague epidemic in a small community in England in 1666 with powerful stories of both fear and courage.

10 Even so, the interest in (and actual subscription to) the promise of cryogenics has risen markedly in my lifetime.

11 Sherwin B. Nuland, *How We Die: Reflections on Life's Final Chapter* (New York: Alfred A. Knopf, 1993), 244.

12 Frank G. Honeycutt, "Jesus Wept—but Why?," *Christian Century*, June 19, 2019, 10.

13 The verb for "greatly disturbed" in these two NRSV verses, *embrimaomai*, means "to snort with anger," conjuring the image of a horse about to break loose in equine agitation.

14 This idea has been attributed to Lutheran theologian William H. Lazareth (1928–2008).

15 Donald Trump, interview with Bob Woodward and Robert Costa, *Washington Post*, April 2, 2016, https://tinyurl.com/ah2xukpm.

16 Geoffrey W. Bromiley, *Theological Dictionary of the New Testament* (Grand Rapids, MI: Eerdmans, 1985), 1274.

17 Bill Wylie Kellerman, ed., *A Keeper of the Word: Selected Writings of William Stringfellow* (Grand Rapids, MI: Eerdmans, 1994), 167, 168.

18 Kellerman, 202 (italics in original).

19 Greek, *peran*; mentioned thirteen times in the four Gospels with five times in Mark alone—4:35, 5:1, 5:21, 6:45, 8:13.

20 The World Council of Churches has used a boat for its promotional symbol since the WCC's inception in 1948.

21 The Greek word for "windstorm" here is the same word used in Job 38:1 (Septuagint) to describe the context for God's famous response to his flummoxed questioner. Mark's use of the word in this sea crossing conjures the limits of Job's interrogation of the divine and sets the scene for Jesus to silence the questioning concerns of the disciples.

22 Note also how the once-naked demoniac becomes "clothed and in his right mind" (5:15), perhaps shaping the use of baptismal garments in the early church, donned prior to first communion. This man's neighbors, posthealing, "were afraid" (5:15) and begged Jesus "to leave their neighborhood" (5:17), a response similar to the aforementioned Philippian Chamber of Commerce and the economic disruption that occurred there.

23 Frank G. Honeycutt, *95 Prostheses: Appendages and Musings for the Body of Christ in Transition* (Eugene, OR: Cascade, 2018), 201.

24 Walter Brueggemann, *Finally Comes the Poet: Daring Speech for Proclamation* (Minneapolis: Fortress, 1989), 114.

25 George Yancy, "Facing the Fact of My Death," *New York Times*, February 3, 2020, https://tinyurl.com/4ane6ydr. This essay introduced a series of monthly interviews in the newspaper with Yancy and twelve religious scholars concerning their understanding of and response to the inevitability of death.

26 *The Farewell*, directed by Lulu Wang (New York: A24 Films, 2019).

27 Mark 16:8, the curious traditional ending of this Gospel, closes with an open-ended sentence in the Greek that brilliantly pulls the reader into the story as a character in the plot.

28 I'm indebted to theologian Ched Myers for this insight.

29 This is how Reginald Fuller translated this German phrase in his English translation called *The Cost of Discipleship*, 2nd ed. (London: SCM, 1959). This translation is noted in *Discipleship*, Dietrich Bonhoeffer Works, vol. 4 (Minneapolis: Fortress, 2003), 87n11. There the phrase is translated, "Every call of Christ leads to death."

30 An interesting contrast: whereas Holy Week attendance in many North American traditions is on the wane, the events of the week, particularly Good Friday, are wildly popular in Central America, suggesting that God's power over death in those troubled countries trumps any reality of fear and violence that seems to hold sway with neighbors to the north.

31 Brian Doyle, *One Long River of Song: Notes on Wonder* (New York: Little, Brown, 2019), 219–20.

Chapter 2

1 In spring of 2020, Edwin accepted a teaching position at Penn State University. We celebrated with a local party.

2 Mark Allan Powell, *Introducing the New Testament: A Historical, Literary, and Theological Survey* (Grand Rapids, MI: Baker Academic, 2009), 359.

3 Timothy F. Lull, ed., *Martin Luther's Basic Theological Writings* (Minneapolis: Fortress, 1989), 640.

4 See my book *Preaching to Skeptics and Seekers* (Nashville: Abingdon, 2001). There I make the case that skeptical acquaintances can be very helpful allies for preachers who desire to link homiletics and authentic evangelism.

5 Ronald P. Byars, *The Sacraments in Biblical Perspective* (Louisville, KY: Westminster John Knox, 2011), 146.

6 Joachim Neander, "Praise to the Lord, the Almighty," in *Evangelical Lutheran Worship* (Minneapolis: Augsburg Fortress, 2006), hymn 858.

7 Gordon T. Smith, *Transforming Conversion: Rethinking the Language and Contours of Christian Initiation* (Grand Rapids, MI: Baker Academic, 2010), 153–54.

8 Scott Gould, *Strangers to Temptation: Stories* (Spartanburg, SC: Hub City Press, 2017), 45.

9 Joseph Heller, *God Knows* (New York: Alfred A. Knopf, 1984), 19.

10 Barbara Brown Taylor, *When God Is Silent* (Lanham, MD: Cowley, 1998), 51.

11 "Holy Baptism," in *Evangelical Lutheran Worship*, 227.

12 I'm indebted to my friend and former teacher, Barbara Lundblad, for this insight.

13 Faith Shearin, "Coffins," in *Telling the Bees* (Nacogdoches, TX: Stephen F. Austin State University Press, 2015), 35.

14 Anthony Doerr, *About Grace* (New York: Penguin, 2004), 360.

Chapter 3

1 See Thomas Lynch, *The Undertaking: Life Studies from the Dismal Trade* (New York: Penguin, 1997), 55–57.

2 Robert G. Hughes, *Preaching Doctrine for the Twenty-First Century* (Minneapolis: Fortress, 1997), 1.

3 Cornelius Plantinga Jr., *Reading for Preaching: The Preacher in Conversation with Storytellers, Biographers, Poets, and Journalists* (Grand Rapids, MI: Eerdmans, 2013), 107.

4 Richard Russo, *Empire Falls* (New York: Vintage, 2001), 177–78.

5 I love the Greek here, as did they: "in a riddle."

6 *Love and Death*, directed by Woody Allen (New York: Jack Rollins & Charles H. Joffe Productions, 1975).

7 See Fea, *Believe Me*.

8 John Leax, *Out Walking: Reflections on Our Place in the Natural World* (Grand Rapids, MI: Baker, 2000), 46.

9 Mark Twain, *Letters from the Earth* (New York: Harper & Row, 1974), 17–18 (italics in original).

10 Rachel Held Evans, *Searching for Sunday: Loving, Leaving, and Finding the Church* (Nashville: Thomas Nelson, 2015), 21.

11 Thomas G. Long, *Accompany Them with Singing: The Christian Funeral* (Louisville, KY: Westminster John Knox, 2009), 108–9.

12 From the Latin *pro* (ahead) and *videre* (to see).

13 Setting the scene, incidentally, of the aforementioned jailing complete with fearless midnight hymn-singing.

14 Karen Russell, "A Temporary Moment in Time," *New Yorker*, April 13, 2020, 36.

15 "You are El-roi," says Hagar in Genesis 16:13—literally, "God who sees."

16 Excerpt from James Parker, "The Coronavirus Prayer," *Atlantic*, April 19, 2020, https://tinyurl.com/yhajtt4j.

17 Lee C. Camp, *Scandalous Witness: A Little Political Manifesto for Christians* (Grand Rapids, MI: Eerdmans, 2020), 98.

18 Lois Phillips Hudson, *The Bones of Plenty* (St. Paul: Minnesota Historical Society Press, 1962), 235.

19 Bret Lott, *Letters and Life: On Being a Writer, on Being a Christian* (Wheaton, IL: Crossway, 2013), 48 (italics in original).

20 O'Connor, "River," 157.

21 Ron Rash, "Their Ancient, Glittering Eyes," in *Chemistry and Other Stories* (New York: Picador, 2007), 1.

22 "A Faithful Imagination," *Christian Century*, April 10, 2019, 7.

23 See John R. Kohlenberger III, *The NRSV Concordance Unabridged* (Grand Rapids, MI: Zondervan, 1991), 1410–12.

24 Cited in Garry Wills, *Font of Life: Ambrose, Augustine, and the Mystery of Baptism* (New York: Oxford University Press, 2012), 126.

25 "Water from Another Time," MP3 audio, track 1 on John McCutcheon, *Gonna Rise Again*, Rounder Records, 1987.

Chapter 4

1 All names in this story have been altered.

2 Kellerman, *Keeper of the Word*, 167.

3 Hampton Sides, *Hellhound on His Trail: The Electrifying Account of the Largest Manhunt in American History* (New York: Anchor, 2011). Sides, an editor-at-large at *Outside* magazine, is an amazing researcher whose books include a biography of Kit Carson and the conquest of the American West (*Blood and Thunder*) and a vivid account of a failed marine voyage to the North Pole in the late nineteenth century (*In the Kingdom of Ice*).

4 James McBride, *The Good Lord Bird* (New York: Riverhead, 2013). McBride—author of *The Color of Water: A Black Man's Tribute to His White Mother*, a highly regarded memoir describing parents of different races—won the National Book Award for his fictional depiction of John Brown.

5 Sides, *Hellhound*, 193–94.

6 McBride, *Good Lord Bird*, 456.

7 Esau McCaulley, "What the Bible Has to Say about Black Anger," *New York Times*, June 14, 2020, https://tinyurl.com/5cwv5zsa.

8 Frank G. Honeycutt, *Jesus and the Family: Crisis and Conversion in the American Household* (Eugene, OR: Cascade, 2013), 38–39 (italics in original).

9 Heidi Neumark, "Sermon in Stone," *Christian Century*, November 3, 2009, 37.

10 Wills, *Font of Life*, 8–9.

11 Robin M. Jensen, *Baptismal Imagery in Early Christianity: Ritual, Visual, and Theological Dimensions* (Grand Rapids, MI: Baker Academic, 2012), 162.

12 Cited in Jensen, 140.

13 See my short book, *Sanctified Living: More Than Grace and Forgiveness* (Minneapolis: Augsburg Fortress, 2008), for a discussion of sanctification from a Lutheran theological perspective.

14 Donald L. Alexander, ed., *Christian Spirituality: Five Views of Sanctification* (Downers Grove, IL: InterVarsity, 1988), 13.

15 Dallas Willard, *The Great Omission: Reclaiming Jesus' Essential Teachings on Discipleship* (San Francisco: HarperOne, 2006), 61.

16 In group settings I've especially used two excellent resources: Will Willimon's short book, *Remember Who You Are: Baptism, a Model for Christian Life* (Nashville: Upper Room, 1998); and Elaine Ramshaw's *The Godparent Book: Ideas and Activities for Godparents and Their Godchildren* (Chicago: Liturgy Training, 1993.)

17 Paul E. Hoffman, *Faith Forming Faith: Bringing New Christians to Baptism and Beyond* (Eugene, OR: Cascade, 2012), 6.

18 Roman Catholics first recovered the catechumenate for use in North American churches through the Rite of Christian Initiation for Adults (RCIA). Episcopalians, Lutherans, and other Protestant bodies soon followed.

19 George G. Hunter III, *How to Reach Secular People* (Nashville: Abingdon, 1992), 41.

20 Names in this and the following two paragraphs have been changed. Each has granted permission to be quoted.

21 Lee C. Camp, *Mere Discipleship: Radical Christianity in a Rebellious World* (Grand Rapids, MI: Brazos, 2008), 152.

22 N. Gordon Cosby, *By Grace Transformed: Christianity for a New Millennium* (New York: Crossroad, 1999), 99–100.

23 Visit the website of the North American Association for the Catechumenate (NAAC) for a variety of resources, including dates for training events: www.journeytobaptism.org.

24 Thomas Merton, *The Seven Storey Mountain* (New York: Harcourt Brace Jovanovich, 1948), 222.

25 Merton, 232.

26 Steve Lundeberg, "Keeping Vigil," *Living Lutheran*, April 2020, 26–27.

27 S. Anita Stauffer, *On Baptismal Fonts: Ancient and Modern* (Piscataway, NJ: Gorgias, 2010), 47 (italics in original).

28 Frederick Buechner, *Wishful Thinking: A Seeker's ABC* (San Francisco: HarperOne, 1993), 6.

29 Will D. Campbell and Richard C. Goode, eds., *Writings on Reconciliation and Resistance* (Eugene, OR: Cascade, 2010), 220.

30 Hoffman, *Faith Forming Faith*, 40 (italics in original).

Chapter 6

1 Will D. Campbell, *Brother to a Dragonfly* (New York: Continuum, 1977), 226.

2 Cited in Anne Lamott, *Bird by Bird: Some Instructions on Writing and Life* (New York: Anchor, 1994), 18.

3 Oliver Whang, "When Virtual Life Turns into Quarantine," *National Geographic*, August 2020, 18.

4 *Lutheran Book of Worship* (Minneapolis: Augsburg, 1978), 66.

5 Luci Shaw, "Our Prayers Break on God," in *Eye of the Beholder* (Orleans, MA: Paraclete, 2018), 70.

6 Randall Kenan, ed., "To Crush a Serpent," in *The Cross of Redemption: Uncollected Writings* (New York: Pantheon, 2010), 160. I'm indebted to my friend, John Lang of Emory and Henry College (VA), for pointing out this Baldwin quote.

7 James K. A. Smith, *On the Road with Saint Augustine: A Real-World Spirituality for Restless Hearts* (Grand Rapids, MI: Brazos, 2019), 73.

Bibliography

Alexander, Donald L., ed. *Christian Spirituality: Five Views of Sanctification.* Downers Grove, IL: InterVarsity, 1988.

Alexander, John F. *Being Church: Reflections on How to Live as the People of God.* Eugene, OR: Cascade, 2012.

Baldwin, James. "To Crush a Serpent." In *The Cross of Redemption: Uncollected Writings,* edited by Randall Kenan, 195–204. New York: Pantheon, 2010.

Bromiley, Geoffrey W. *Theological Dictionary of the New Testament.* Grand Rapids, MI: Eerdmans, 1985.

Brueggemann, Walter. *Finally Comes the Poet: Daring Speech for Proclamation.* Minneapolis: Fortress, 1989.

Buechner, Frederick. *Wishful Thinking: A Seeker's ABC.* San Francisco: HarperOne, 1993.

Byars, Ronald P. *The Sacraments in Biblical Perspective.* Louisville, KY: Westminster John Knox, 2011.

Camp, Lee C. *Mere Discipleship: Radical Christianity in a Rebellious World.* Grand Rapids, MI: Brazos, 2003.

———. *Scandalous Witness: A Little Political Manifesto for Christians.* Grand Rapids, MI: Eerdmans, 2020.

Campbell, Will D. *Brother to a Dragonfly.* New York: Continuum, 1977.

Campbell, Will D., and Richard C. Goode, ed. *Writings on Reconciliation and Resistance.* Eugene, OR: Cascade, 2010.

Clapp, Rodney. *A Peculiar People: The Church as Culture in a Post-Christian Society.* Downers Grove, IL: InterVarsity, 1996.

Coppins, McKay. "The 2020 Disinformation War." *Atlantic,* March 2020.

Cosby, N. Gordon. *By Grace Transformed: Christianity for a New Millennium*. New York: Crossroad, 1999.

Doyle, Brian. *One Long River of Song: Notes on Wonder*. New York: Little, Brown, 2019.

Evangelical Lutheran Worship. Minneapolis: Augsburg Fortress, 2006.

Evans, Rachel Held. *Searching for Sunday: Loving, Leaving, and Finding the Church*. Nashville: Nelson, 2015.

"A Faithful Imagination." *Christian Century*, April 10, 2019.

Fea, John. *Believe Me: The Evangelical Road to Donald Trump*. Grand Rapids, MI: Eerdmans, 2018.

Finn, Thomas M. "Baptismal Death and Resurrection: A Study in Fourth Century Eastern Baptismal Theology." *Worship* 43, no. 3 (March 1969): 175–189.

———. *Early Christian Baptism and the Catechumenate: Italy, North Africa, and Egypt*. Collegeville, MN: Liturgical Press, 1992.

Hartnell, Jack. *Medieval Bodies: Life and Death in the Middle Ages*. New York: W. W. Norton, 2018.

Hoffman, Paul E. *Faith Forming Faith: Bringing New Christians to Baptism and Beyond*. Eugene, OR: Cascade, 2012.

Honeycutt, Frank G. "Buried with Christ: Baptism Is about Dying." *Christian Century*, August 14, 2019.

———. *Jesus and the Family: Crisis and Conversion in the American Household*. Eugene, OR: Cascade, 2013.

———. "Jesus Wept—but Why?" *Christian Century*, June 19, 2019.

———. "The Lure of Express Conversion." In *What Do You Seek? Welcoming the Adult Inquirer*, edited by Dennis Bushkofsky, 15–23. Minneapolis: Augsburg Fortress, 2000.

———. *95 Prostheses: Appendages and Musings for the Body of Christ in Transition*. Eugene, OR: Cascade, 2018.

———. *The Truth Shall Make You Odd: Speaking with Pastoral Integrity in Awkward Situations*. Grand Rapids, MI: Brazos, 2011.

Huck, Gabe. *How Can I Keep from Singing? Thoughts about Liturgy for Musicians*. Chicago: Liturgy Training, 1989.

Hughes, Robert G. *Preaching Doctrine for the Twenty-First Century.* Minneapolis: Fortress, 1997.

Hunter, George G., III. *How to Reach Secular People.* Nashville: Abingdon, 1992.

Jensen, Robin M. *Baptismal Imagery in Early Christianity: Ritual, Visual, and Theological Dimensions.* Grand Rapids, MI: Baker Academic, 2012.

————. "Christian Community, Sacred Space, and the Liturgy." *Arts in Religious and Theological Studies* 12, no. 1 (2000): 7–13.

Kellerman, Bill Wylie, ed. *A Keeper of the Word: Selected Writings of William Stringfellow.* Grand Rapids, MI: Eerdmans, 1994.

Kohlenberger, John R., III. *The NRSV Concordance Unabridged.* Grand Rapids, MI: Zondervan, 1991.

Kolb, Robert, and Timothy J. Wengert, eds. *The Book of Concord: The Confessions of the Evangelical Lutheran Church.* Minneapolis: Fortress, 2000.

Lamott, Anne. *Bird by Bird: Some Instructions on Writing and Life.* New York: Anchor, 1994.

Leax, John. *Out Walking: Reflections on Our Place in the Natural World.* Grand Rapids, MI: Baker, 2000.

Long, Thomas G. *Accompany Them with Singing: The Christian Funeral.* Louisville, KY: Westminster John Knox, 2009.

————. *What Shall We Say? Evil, Suffering, and the Crisis of Faith.* Grand Rapids, MI: Eerdmans, 2011.

Lott, Bret. *Letters and Life: On Being a Writer, on Being a Christian.* Wheaton, IL: Crossway, 2013.

Lull, Timothy F., ed. *Martin Luther's Basic Theological Writings.* Minneapolis: Fortress, 1989.

Lundeberg, Steve. "Keeping Vigil." *Living Lutheran,* April 15, 2020.

Lutheran Book of Worship. Minneapolis: Augsburg, 1978.

Lynch, Thomas. *The Undertaking: Life Studies from the Dismal Trade.* New York: Penguin, 1997.

Marsh, Abigail. "How We Can Keep Fear from Spiraling Out of Our Control." *Washington Post*, June 23, 2020. https://tinyurl.com/8ja33rc.

McCaulley, Esau. "What the Bible Has to Say about Black Anger." *New York Times*, June 14, 2020. https://tinyurl.com/5cwv5zsa.

McKnight, Scot. *It Takes a Church to Baptize: What the Bible Says about Infant Baptism.* Grand Rapids, MI: Brazos, 2018.

———. *Pastor Paul: Nurturing a Culture of Christoformity in the Church.* Grand Rapids, MI: Brazos, 2019.

Merton, Thomas. *The Seven Storey Mountain.* New York: Harcourt Brace Jovanovich, 1948.

Morand, Amelia. "Lessons in Craft with David James Duncan." CutBank, February 13, 2019. https://tinyurl.com/r3e2hmyw.

Motlagh, Jason. "No Way Out." *National Geographic*, March 2019.

Neumark, Heidi. "Sermon in Stone." *Christian Century*, November 3, 2009.

Norris, Kathleen. *The Cloister Walk.* New York: Riverhead, 1996.

Nuland, Sherwin B. *How We Die: Reflections on Life's Final Chapter.* New York: Alfred A. Knopf, 1993.

O'Connor, Flannery. "The Fiction Writer and His Country." In *Literature for Composition: Essays, Fiction, Poetry, and Drama*, edited by Sylvan Barnet, Morton Berman, William Burto, William E. Cain, and Marcia Stubbs, 1253–1254. Upper Saddle River, NJ: Prentice Hall, 2000.

Parker, James. "The Coronavirus Prayer." *Atlantic*, April 19, 2020. https://tinyurl.com/yhajtt4j.

Pinker, Steven. *The Better Angels of Our Nature: Why Violence Has Declined.* New York: Viking, 2011.

Plantinga, Cornelius. *Reading for Preaching: The Preacher in Conversation with Storytellers, Biographers, Poets, and Journalists.* Grand Rapids, MI: Eerdmans, 2013.

Powell, Mark Allan. *Introducing the New Testament: A Historical, Literary, and Theological Survey.* Grand Rapids, MI: Baker Academic, 2009.

Ramshaw, Elaine. *The Godparent Book: Ideas and Activities for Godparents and Their Godchildren.* Chicago: Liturgy Training, 1993.

Russell, Karen. "A Temporary Moment in Time." *New Yorker,* April 13, 2020.

Sides, Hampton. *Hellhound on His Trail: The Electrifying Account of the Largest Manhunt in American History.* New York: Anchor, 2010.

Smith, Gordon T. *Transforming Conversion: Rethinking the Language and Contours of Christian Initiation.* Grand Rapids, MI: Baker Academic, 2010.

Smith, James K. A. *On the Road with Saint Augustine: A Real-World Spirituality for Restless Hearts.* Grand Rapids, MI: Brazos, 2019.

Stauffer, Anita S. *On Baptismal Fonts: Ancient and Modern.* Piscataway, NJ: Gorgias, 2010.

Stone, Bryan. *Evangelism after Christendom: The Theology and Practice of Christian Witness.* Grand Rapids, MI: Brazos, 2007.

Taylor, Barbara Brown. *When God Is Silent.* Lanham, MD: Cowley, 1998.

Thompson, Clifford. *What It Is: Race, Family, and One Thinking Black Man's Blues.* New York: Other Press, 2019.

Westerhoff, John. *Bringing Up Children in the Christian Faith.* Minneapolis: Winston, 1980.

Whang, Oliver. "When Virtual Life Turns into Quarantine." *National Geographic,* August 2020.

Willard, Dallas. *The Great Omission: Reclaiming Jesus' Essential Teachings on Discipleship.* San Francisco: HarperOne, 2006.

Willimon, William H. *Remember Who You Are: Baptism, a Model for Christian Life.* Nashville: Upper Room, 1980.

Wills, Garry. *Font of Life: Ambrose, Augustine, and the Mystery of Baptism.* New York: Oxford University Press, 2012.

Yancy, George. "Facing the Fact of My Death." *New York Times,* February 3, 2020. https://tinyurl.com/4ane6ydr.

Fiction

Brooks, Geraldine. *Year of Wonders: A Novel of the Plague*. New York: Penguin, 2001.

Doerr, Anthony. *About Grace*. New York: Penguin, 2004.

Duncan, Glen. *I, Lucifer*. New York: Grove, 2002.

Gould, Scott. *Strangers to Temptation: Stories*. Spartanburg, SC: Hub City Press, 2017.

Heller, Joseph. *God Knows*. New York: Alfred A. Knopf, 1984.

Hudson, Lois Phillips. *The Bones of Plenty*. St. Paul: Minnesota Historical Society Press, 1962.

Lewis, C. S. *The Voyage of the Dawn Treader*. New York: Macmillan, 1952.

McBride, James. *The Good Lord Bird*. New York: Riverhead, 2013.

McDermott, Alice. *The Ninth Hour*. New York: Farrar, Straus and Giroux, 2017.

O'Connor, Flannery. *The Complete Stories*. New York: Farrar, Straus and Giroux, 1984.

Rash, Ron. *Chemistry and Other Stories*. New York: Picador, 2007.

Russo, Richard. *Empire Falls*. New York: Vintage, 2001.

Twain, Mark. *Letters from the Earth*. New York: Harper & Row, 1938.

Films

Allen, Woody, dir. *Love and Death*. New York: Jack Rollins & Charles H. Joffe Productions, 1975.

Wang, Lulu, dir. *The Farewell*. New York: A24 Films, 2019.

Poetry

Shaw, Luci. *Eye of the Beholder*. Orleans, MA: Paraclete, 2018.

Shearin, Faith. *Telling the Bees*. Nacogdoches, TX: Stephen F. Austin State University Press, 2015.